"Sean has inspired me for years, so much so that I even wrote about him in my book. The reason why I love and respect my good buddy is he truly gets it—he lives in harmony! In this book he gives you timeless wisdom in a fun, loving, and modern-day voice that you'll enjoy rereading for the rest of your life."

—**James Arthur Ray,** author, *Harmonic Wealth*;
coauthor, *The Secret*

"As a writer it takes a lot for a book to impress me—and a lot more for a book to impact me. *Get Off Your "But"* did *both!* Simply put, Sean silences the voice that tells us we're not enough."

—**Steven Pressfield,** author, *The War of Art*

"The reason why some people never win at the game of life is they're too busy sitting on their BUTS on the sideline instead of *standing* on the field making history! Perseverance is the name of the game, whether you're running a business, a family, or making the cut for the Notre Dame football team. *Get Off Your "But"* is the perfect book to strengthen your perseverance and lead you to the ultimate victories in life!"

—**Rudy Ruettiger,** inspiration for the movie "Rudy";
author, *Rudy's Insights for Winning in Life*

"If you've ever been afraid of meeting someone, dating someone, or starting a conversation with someone you wanted to meet, and you'd like to *destroy* those fears, then read this book. I guarantee that the material inside will get you the results you want from life . . ."

—**David DeAngelo,** author, *Double Your Dating*

"No ifs, ands, or BUTS about it. Sean sets an awesome example of someone who could find every reason to give up. This book offers inspiration, humor, and insights on overcoming mental barriers that could rent space in your head!"

—**Gary Coxe,** author, *Don't Let Others Rent Space in Your Head*

"Have you ever felt stuck in life? If so I'd recommend you read this book. Sean lays out in a very entertaining manner a set of tools for us to deal with challenging circumstances. While he might not be able to walk, he truly embodies the idea that anything is possible if you take it one step at a time."

—**Robert Maurer, Ph.D.,** author, *One Small Step*

"Sean is an inspiration showing like no one else what perseverance and the raw power of belief can accomplish. He has imbued this book with an extraordinary message he puts into action every day. Read it—you won't be disappointed."

—**Ray Dodd,** author, *BeliefWorks* and *The Power of Belief*

"Sean's book is a touching, surefire approach to stop your excuses from controlling your life; and even more important, to stop putting off the life you dream of."

—**Rita Emmett,** author, *The Procrastinator's Handbook* and *The Clutter-Busting Handbook*

"Sean Stephenson is a human re-frame. The moment his story and passion connect with you, life looks different, and your excuses are out the window."

—**Steve Chandler,** author, *The Story of You*

Get Off YOUR "But"

How to End Self-Sabotage and Stand Up for Yourself

Sean Stephenson

Foreword by
Anthony Robbins

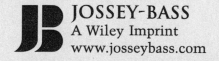

JOSSEY-BASS
A Wiley Imprint
www.josseybass.com

Library of Congress Cataloging-in-Publication Data

Stephenson, Sean.
    Get off your "but": how to end self-sabotage and stand up for yourself / by Sean Stephenson.
        p. cm.
    ISBN 978-0-470-39993-4 (cloth)
        1. Success. 2. Self-defeating behavior. 3. Nurturing behavior. I. Title.
    BF637.S8S69285   2009
    650.1—dc22

                                                              2008041491

Printed in the United States of America

FIRST EDITION

HB Printing 10 9 8 7 6 5 4 3 2

CONTENTS

To fears, excuses, and insecurities.

If it weren't for you, I would be out of a job.

Be forewarned though—I plan on eradicating you from this planet.

Your days are numbered.

ACKNOWLEDGMENTS

To Mom, Dad, and Heidi—thanks for all your love and support, and for asking a million times the most annoying question ever, "Is your book done yet?"

To my amazing pit crew—you know who you are. You're the reason I'm in first place!

To my powerful mentors and "friendtors"—thanks for teaching me the things that I needed to learn, saying the things I may not have wanted to hear but needed to, and believing in me on the days I didn't believe in myself.

To Bryn Freedman—thanks for seeing things in me other people couldn't. I love ya, partner.

To Alice Martell—thanks for finding the perfect publisher and kindly answering all my extremely naive questions.

To Tony Robbins—thanks for carrying me across the coals in life.

To Dr. Robert Young—thanks for making me unbreakable.

To Eben Pagan—thanks for proving to me that I am capable of creating attraction. And thanks for being one of the most giving mentors I have.

To President Clinton—thanks for teaching me the power of connection.

To William O. Lipinski—thanks for teaching me how to network.

To Alan Rinzler and Naomi Luchs Sigal—thanks for making me sound as though I know what I'm talking about here.

To Phi Kappa Theta, the American Legion, Lyons Township High School, DePaul University, Shriners and Chicago Children's Hospitals, and the Make-A-Wish Foundation—your presence shaped the course of my destiny.

To the entire Stephenson and Clinch extended families—thanks for all the prayers; God heard you. Keep them coming.

FOREWORD
Anthony Robbins

I have dedicated my time here on earth to finding the tools that can help each of us experience an extraordinary quality of life. I do believe that such a life can only be found by living one's true passion. Without passion, an individual gets caught in the trap of making a living instead of designing a life. When we fall into the trap of getting up each day to reenact an "ordinary" existence, we find ourselves at a level that is merely one of survival. Thus, I have spent more than a quarter of a century traveling the globe, learning from and teaching individuals the importance of living life at the level we're made for! One of the blessings of teaching so many people is getting to meet some incredible human beings. In 1998, I made friends with one such person, Sean Stephenson—a little man with such a big spirit, it could move mountains. His smile and loving nature were truly infectious.

Sean came to me through the help of the Make-A-Wish Foundation. He wanted me to mentor him because, although his life was filled with accomplishments and joy, so too was it filled with frustration, pain, and a fight for survival. His face was covered in acne. Because of his genetic bone disorder, his back was riddled with pain, and his bones were so brittle that they were fracturing constantly. Doctors felt that Sean's condition would most likely turn fatal—with a premature death. One could see that his entire body lacked the energy and vitality it deserved. I told Sean exactly whom to see and what to do. He took immediate and massive action by changing his entire diet and lifestyle. This action turned Sean's physiology around 180 degrees. His acne, chronic back pain, and bone fractures disappeared completely, and they haven't returned since. His prognosis is no longer premature death. Believe it or not, Sean now body-builds and has a six-pack set of abs that most fitness competitors dream of.

The way a person lives his life can either serve as a warning or as an example to us. Sean is the example! An example of how to get over your fears, insecurities, and excuses. Sean could have sentenced himself to a lifetime of misery, yet he consciously chose to pardon himself from the pity. Sean amazes me not because he overcame his struggles, but because he chose to dedicate his life to helping others do the same. He doesn't just have a compelling story to tell in this book; he has a specific plan for you to follow. His plan is designed to help you and people you care about to get off what he calls your BUTS. Of course, in Sean's own words, he's referring to our

BUT fears (BUT what if I fail . . .)

BUT insecurities (BUT I'm not good enough . . .)

BUT excuses (BUT there's no time . . .)

This book will show you how to move beyond your limitations and begin to experience and share your gifts at the highest level. Both Sean and I STAND for the possibility of you living at the level of the extraordinary. Read this book in its entirety, follow the lessons closely, and watch as your life transforms into a masterpiece filled with an abundance of bliss, passion, and gratitude.

Live with passion!

Anthony Robbins
Author, *Awaken the Giant Within*
and *Unlimited Power*

Get Off
YOUR "But"

BORN TO KICK BUT
The Short Story of a Big Life

Most parents pray that their baby will come out with all ten toes and ten fingers. And I did! Except they were all broken.

As I made my entry into the world on May 5, 1979, the sudden silence of the doctors in the delivery room said it all: we've got trouble. Something was drastically wrong. My arms and legs flopped around like a rag doll's. The crown of my head was not just mildly misshapen from the pressure of the birth canal; it looked like a deformed piece of Silly Putty. As the doctors would soon learn, almost every bone in my tiny body had been crushed by the stress of being born. They told my parents to prepare for the worst: "There's a good chance Sean will die within twenty-four hours."

The doctors quickly determined that I had been born with a genetic disorder that caused my bones to be incredibly brittle. The slightest touch could break my bones, so they ordered that no one should touch me or hold me close. For the first few weeks of my life, I was kept immobilized in the intensive care unit of Chicago's Children's Hospital.

I was not a happy camper. My cries were not those of a fussy baby in need of a quick poopy-diaper change, but blood-curdling cries of pain. I like to say now that I was being considerate—I cried during only two long periods of the day: when the sun was up and when it was down.

Brittle Bones

Birth had not been good to me. X-rays showed that it would be quicker to count the number of bones that *weren't* broken in my body than those that were. To contain the massive trauma, doctors built a tiny cast that encased most of my body, and propped me on a pillow with my arms and legs sticking straight out. The nurses announced that I looked like King Tut on his throne—the Field Museum had opened its King Tut exhibit just that month. Could I be the reincarnated soul of an ancient Egyptian VIP? The return of the pharaoh's spirit remains purely speculative, but he and I did turn out to have one thing in common: despite the pain of my birth and first days on earth, my life would be filled with adventures fit for a king.

The doctors explained to my parents that I had been born with Osteogenesis Imperfecta, commonly called OI or brittle bones disorder. My mom and dad could hardly pronounce it, let alone fathom the endless challenges it would present for them. Those challenges started on the day of my birth. They couldn't swaddle me up in a cute little blanket and take me home to the nursery they had prepared for my arrival, or let my big sister, Heidi, cuddle me. No, they had to leave me in a sterile room in the care of (almost) complete strangers.

My Parents Didn't Sit on Their BUTS

After the delivery, my mother lay in a hospital bed all by herself. She had been told to grieve, either for the impending loss of her baby—I might die at any minute—or for the ongoing loss of not having a "normal" baby. My parents were told that I would never grow up physically, that my growth would be permanently stunted. My bones would be as fragile as glass: little—even *no*—impact could cause them to break. The stress of a sneeze could shatter my ribs.

And then a nurse came into my mom's room with a really big hypodermic.

"What's this for?" my mom asked.

"To dry up your mother's milk."

"What would I want to do that for?"

"Well," said the nurse, holding the syringe in the air and preparing to inject it, "why would you want to nurse a baby like *that*?"

I'm surprised my mom didn't grab the needle and stab the nurse. Needless to say, my mom refused the shot. Then she and my dad began to refuse many other things. Their greatest gift to me was refusing to lose faith in my survival.

They never thought about me in a negative way—not once. They never said, "We would be happy about the birth of our son . . . BUT he is never going to be normal." In fact, they weren't compelled in the *slightest* to sit back on their BUTS! They never stopped loving me exactly as I was, then and now. They never lost faith that I was okay and was going to survive. They never succumbed to any doubt or ambivalence about me as a human being, their son. They never thought, "Sure, Sean's a great kid, BUT . . ." They never gave up on me.

My mom went home, and pumped breast milk. My dad visited me in the hospital in the city every day to feed me the tiny bottles of Mom's milk that she had sent with love from home. And I didn't die—in fact, despite the odds, I was more and more ready to live. I owed my fighting spirit to my parents, who from day one were solidly committed to seeing me survive, succeed, and develop into a powerful force on this planet.

It wasn't an easy road to travel, when taking even one step could break my leg.

Growing Up the Hard Way

While other kids my age were progressing from squirming to crawling to wobbling to walking, I went from not moving at all to my own take on crawling. My family called it "scootching." This maneuver, which entailed alternately shifting my shoulders and rear, was like an army crawl—very flat to the ground, except on my back. At first, I moved about as quickly as a moderately fast snail. Eventually, when I developed the muscles to log-roll my body around the house, I achieved a much quicker land speed.

Sitting up—a milestone for other babies—was beyond my capabilities. At that time, my muscle structure was not developed enough to sit myself up from a lying-down position. I was shocked the first time I saw someone with my condition prop himself upright on his own. That "Aha!" moment occurred a few years later, at Chicago's Shriners Hospital, where I received regular medical treatment. There, I came face-to-face with someone whose physical appearance actually resembled mine! I had spent my whole life around "normal-looking" people, so to finally see someone who was my height, used a wheelchair, and actually had the exact same facial features was both startling and overwhelming. Imagine living your whole life on a planet where everyone is ten feet tall and has green skin. Then one day you turn the corner and you're toe to toe with someone your own height and your own skin color. It was a huge revelation and a huge relief.

My years in and out of hospitals also gave me an important insight: other people had problems too. I learned that there were far more debilitating conditions than mine. I saw a man who had to endure the agonizing pain of third-degree burns over most of his body. There were people paralyzed from the neck down, who could only breathe on ventilators. Some children had immune systems so chaotic they couldn't leave the sterile hospital environment. At least I had feeling and movement throughout my body.

All the major systems in my body (digestive, respiratory, cardiovascular, reproductive, and so on) worked just fine. It was the other stuff—the everyday parts most people take for granted—that were a problem for me. For example, a small but crucial challenge I faced when I was growing up was reaching the top of my head. My arms have never been long enough. And though that might not sound like a big deal, it is. Putting on a baseball cap, brushing my hair, or—more important—scratching an annoying itch were all out of the question without the assistance of others.

Standing was also out of the question. I've never had the bone density to support my body in a standing position, so walking has never been possible. Even if I could support the weight on my legs, I still couldn't walk, because my muscles are more developed and stronger than my bones. Over the years, they have bent and twisted my legs into a permanent position that makes walking impossible.

Before that happened, though, surgeons had attempted to straighten my legs by inserting metal rods. Unfortunately, my body rejected the rods, actually forcing them right out of my bones over a period of months. The most intense sensation of physical pain I've ever experienced was the day the doctors removed a rod from my left leg. They gave me just a topical anesthetic to prep the skin for the incision, and told me it wouldn't hurt that bad. Uh-huh. Right!

I'll never forget it. They took hold of the tip of the rod that was already poking out of the bone and began to pull. A scalding hot rrripp! shot up my leg and straight into the base of my brain. It felt as if someone were turning my leg inside out, as if they'd inserted a giant vacuum cleaner into my kneecap and sucked out my entire lower leg bone.

From that moment on, I had no interest in getting another rod put into my body, especially because it wouldn't have improved my chances of walking or made me any taller. I basically reached my full height—three feet tall—in about the third grade, and haven't grown since.

My "Costumized" Wheelchair

I've had four wheelchairs in my life—five, if you count the super-sporty, low-profile, turquoise green racing chair that I use for exercise. But even the regular ones got way more interesting from time to time.

My parents soon became very creative with my wheelchairs. They built me great floats—an elaborate cardboard "costume" we put around my chair for me to show off three times a year: Halloween, Fourth of July parades, and in our yearly hometown Pet Parade. We built everything from train engines, race cars, tractors, steam shovels, and motorcycle sidecars to pirate ships and mummy coffins.

I spent three-quarters of my day in a wheelchair at school and hanging out at my friends' houses. The remaining quarter of every day I would lie on the floor of my house to rest my back muscles—they were exhausted from keeping me upright.

Learning from Pain

I had extreme back pain practically every day until I turned eighteen years old. I spent a large part of my childhood stuck indoors with excruciating pain. This gave me a lot of time to explore the workings of my mind. I didn't read books about human behavior. I just naturally picked up on meditation, visualization, and mind-body healing techniques out of sheer necessity to deal with the pain.

No one told me the technical terms for what I was doing to displace pain from my conscious mind. No one gave me the seven steps to highly effective coping, or taught me how to hypnotize myself into accepting my condition with an open heart. It wasn't until years later that I realized that much of what I learned through self-discovery as a child was right on the money.

Pain was my teacher, and I became its good little student.

Cause and Effect

Every toddler learns the meaning of causality—if I do this, I will cause that. For most kids, it's about dropping a toy on the floor or touching a hot stove and getting burned. For me, the equation was a little different: if I try to lift a heavy object, my arm will snap.

My brain quickly became wired to recognize that it needed to be always alert, to be always on the lookout for what could happen next. I needed to pay attention to things that other kids would never have to concern themselves with. What if someone comes walking quickly around the corner and bumps into me? What if that heavy lunchbox perched on the corner of the desk comes crashing down on me? What if this guy next to me tries to grab my arm and shake it too hard? My mind was constantly scanning the environment for any possible danger. This caution saved me on many occasions, but I was still a kid—and kids sometimes get excited and forget to think. One particular Halloween, in 1988, I forgot all about caution and thinking. But I'll never forget what happened.

I was in the fourth grade, and it was Halloween morning, right before school. My mom was in the kitchen packing my lunch. I was in the living room lying on the floor with a big smile on my face. This was my favorite day of the year. Sure, I liked Christmas, my birthday, and all the other holidays. But Halloween held a special place in my heart.

To most kids Halloween meant candy, parties, and wearing costumes. To me, Halloween was real magic—a disappearing act. Every day of my life—my entire life—I had been stared at because I looked so different. Strangers would point, scowl, and sometimes even laugh at my appearance. No matter what time I left my house or where I was,

I couldn't escape it. The one thing I wanted so badly to do as a child was just put on a baseball cap, mix into a crowd of people, and disappear. That, however, was never an option . . .

Except on Halloween!

On that one day, *everyone* got dressed up, *everyone* looked different, and I got to blend in. I absolutely loved it.

On this Halloween morning, when I was nine years old, Mom finished packing my lunch and was taking my stuff out to the car. I was so excited, I just couldn't keep still. I was going as a mummy, and, already wearing my costume, I started rolling around on the floor out of my chair.

"Oh," I thought to myself, "I look so good! I can't wait to show this off to my friends."

I rolled all over the floor, filled with joy and impatient to get going . . . and then my left leg caught on the corner of the door frame and bent back. *Snap!*

The world stood still. I knew what would happen next. There was always a delay between hearing the snap and feeling the pain. In a fraction of a second it felt as though my whole life came crumbling down.

I'd broken my femur, the big bone in my thigh. My temperature began to rise, and sweat burned into my eyes. My breathing became ragged. It felt as if somebody had put a vise on the bone and was twisting it, tighter and tighter.

As if the pain weren't enough, white-hot anger exploded in my mind. It coursed through my veins and drilled right to my heart. This was not fair! I was being punished for a crime I had never committed.

So I let out a blood-curdling scream.

"WHY MEEEEEEEEEEEEEEEEEEEEEEEEEEEEEE? WHAT DID I EVER DO TO DESERVE THIS?"

Mom came running into the room and knelt down beside me. She knew the drill. There was little she could do to help me. She couldn't race me to the hospital—there was nothing the doctors could do either. The medical experts had told her early on that all she could do was keep me immobilized on the very spot where I had broken the bone for four to six weeks, until I healed. *Literally* the same spot. It didn't matter whether it was my bedroom, the basement, or the living room floor, that's where I had to remain— absolutely still—until the bone healed. Eating, drinking, and even going to the bathroom had to be modified so that I could do it all from that spot.

Mom tried to calm me down. "Shhhhhhh . . . Sean . . . sweetie, we have to relax."

Then, as she always did, Mom tried playing this little game with me to transport my mind as far away from the pain as possible.

"Sean, what was your favorite part about our last vacation?"

But that Halloween day I didn't want to play any games. I knew I was going to be stuck indoors on the one day of the year that meant the most to me. I was furious, and my mom could see that in my eyes. She stopped playing, leaned back, and formulated a question—a question that would change the course of my life.

Mom ran her fingers through my sweaty hair and looked deep into my eyes. "Sean," she asked quietly, "is this going to be a gift or a burden?"

A gift? A gift? Gifts come on your birthday. You open them up and say, "Woo hoo!" Was she crazy?

But before I could say anything, something magical happened. Something I can't explain with science. My calling and purpose in life came and found me. It was as though a warm wind of wisdom came whirling into my living room and surrounded my body.

Whooooosshhhhhhhh!

Finding the Purpose of My Life

In that moment, in the fourth grade, on the living room floor, in terrible pain, I had a clear revelation: I had always loved my life, amid all the pain. And—here's the really important part—I realized that I was meant to teach others how to do the same.

Then Mom shared another profound thought with me.

"Sean," she said, "pain is inevitable. Eventually, it touches us all. Suffering, however, is optional."

I've never been the same since. That Halloween day, I received a gift that lifted the anger from my body and gave me a reason never to give up. Sure, I've been sad. But it's the temporary kind of sadness, not the total despair I had sometimes felt before that Halloween lying on the floor, and that I sometimes see in the eyes of others.

A Different Kind of Pain

As the years went by, I racked up bone fractures like other boys racked up Boy Scout merit badges. We lost count after two hundred. And the broken bones derailed more than just Halloween. They canceled vacations, sleepovers, talent shows, science fairs, and hundreds of days of school.

I've been asked on many occasions, "Sean, don't you get used to the pain after a while?"

"No," I reply, "at best, I understand how to control it."

Surprisingly, the physical pain of my condition has not been as torturous as the emotional pain. I remember many days when I'd sit at the window of my homeroom class, wiping my eyes and watching my friends playing dodgeball and freeze tag at recess on the playground down below. Often, I'd pray for rain. Rain meant that recess had to be indoors, and I could be with all my friends, playing Nintendo, Legos, Uno . . . games my fragile little body could handle. They were great for bonding with my friends, but those games weren't always enough to keep my rambunctious buddies inside with me. I often felt pretty isolated.

I did have my sister, though. But sometimes, having me for a brother made her life hard.

"Sean's Sister"

My sister, Heidi, was only two years old when I came into the picture and turned her world upside down. One of the nurses in the hospital told my parents, "Don't worry about

Sean; he'll be all right. Make sure you give plenty of love and attention to Heidi, or she'll be the one who will be overshadowed by his disability."

My parents took this advice to heart, and always went out of their way to make sure Heidi got as much attention as I did. The rest of the world, however, didn't follow that line of reasoning. People were concerned about my health and my pain, and were constantly asking, "How's Sean?" My parents would politely reply, "Heidi and Sean are great; thanks for asking!"

Of course, it didn't help my relationship with my sister that I was this adorable little freckle-faced kid with a smile that could charm a cobra. I was also radically outgoing, and never stopped socializing with the world. Everyone knew me everywhere I went in my town. Although Heidi always won the leads in the school musicals and got good grades, the massive amount of attention I received just for being different often stole her well-deserved thunder. She hated being labeled "Sean's sister."

For the most part, though, our sibling rivalry was no different than anyone else's, except that we had to deal with the added component of my physical condition. I can only imagine that it was a difficult time for her. But today, as adults, we are extremely close.

My Limiting Belief

Even though I knew the condition of my body was an unchangeable act of a divine reason I would never fully understand, I still wanted to run, jump, and climb like my friends. As I got older, these playful childish desires were replaced by new yearnings—and with them came loads of new disappointments.

In 1991, when I entered junior high school, my world opened up to the most mysterious element on the planet: girls! I loved them for more than just the hormonal reasons. Like me, they were really social and made great companions. As I was growing up, I always had girlfriends—that is, until "the note."

When I was in the seventh grade, I was head-over-wheels for this one girl in the eighth grade who was beautiful and super cool—and she liked me too. I believe that no matter what age you are, for a male there is no greater feeling than knowing that a girl you like likes you. I had that. I was the envy of all the guys in the school. I was the king of the world . . . until the day I opened my locker and found the note. Not just any note. It was a piece of paper that would haunt my self-image for another twelve years.

"Sean," it said, "we have to break up. My girlfriends said I shouldn't be dating a guy like you. I'm sorry."

What did she mean? She can't date a guy who's funny, nice, and knows all the words to Vanilla Ice's music? *What?* I wasn't satisfied with this unclear message. So I sent out my spy, Katy, a cousin of mine who went to the same school. What she found out stole the glow from my heart and left me with a secret resentment toward women from which I didn't fully recover until my mid-twenties.

"Sean, I hate to be the one who tells you this…" Katy stopped, apprehensive. I guess she knew I'd be upset.

"Just say it!" I shouted.

"She said that she really likes you, BUT all her friends were making fun of her for dating a little guy in a wheelchair. They told her she could do so much better."

"Oh."

A sudden wave of shame and sadness filled up my lungs; I could barely breathe. I'd felt pain before, but nothing like this! I fought back the tears until I found an empty classroom I could hide in. I must have cried for an hour straight. I even turned my wheelchair so I couldn't see my own reflection in the windows. I was humiliated. I thought my rib cage was going to implode from the empty feeling in my chest.

My condition had kept me from athletics, from boyish explorations of the woods, and now it was isolating me from love. I made a critical mistake that day when I hid in the biology room, a mistake that locked up my heart for years.

I formed this limiting belief: "You are flawed. You are a nice guy, BUT that will never be enough for girls to love and want you."

Ugly thought, huh? I know.

It didn't keep me from asking out girls, but none of the dating relationships I attempted in high school, college, and even a few years out of college ever worked. I was always waiting in fear for the girl to "wake up" and see she could do better. I dragged this horrific mind-set into the lives of more women than I care to remember. And of course I kept attracting the type of woman who fell for me but was eventually compelled to dump me because of what her friends thought.

Still, my life wasn't all bad. In fact, it was about to get much better.

The Promise of Good Things to Come

Many adults like to look at their childhood as if it were an experience that happened a long time ago, when they were silly and naive, and didn't know any better. Yet many experts would argue that our childhood is the blueprint for the "design" of the person we are today. Fortunately, when I entered high school in 1993, I began to develop in a positive way, which brought the promise of good things to come.

My parents did a tremendous job in raising me and my sister. It seemed as if they always had just the right things to say to us. One nugget of wisdom that empowered me through most of my teens was this: "Sean, there are many things you won't be able to do in life because of your physical condition, so get busy finding the things you *can* do."

As my body entered puberty, my bone fractures diminished. I went from missing seventy and eighty days of school a year to missing only thirty or forty, which gave me more of an opportunity to participate in extracurricular activities. I gravitated toward two areas of interest: television production and student government.

My high school, Lyons Township, in La Grange, Illinois, was so large it was separated into two different campuses. The freshmen and sophomores were at one campus, the juniors and seniors were at another, and both campuses were only about a mile away from where I grew up. The high school actually had its own radio and TV stations, and I latched on to both of them as an outlet to express my creativity. Over four years of high school, I produced talk shows, dating shows, political commentaries, and a television sitcom series.

I actually wrote, produced, edited, cast, and sometimes even starred in my sitcom—seven episodes over the course of my sophomore year. We had more than twenty-five actors and actresses, and filmed on location in the school, as well as at dozens of off-campus locations for which we never had permits and had to shoot fast. The show was called Living Through High School, and it had quite a following on our town's cable access channel. It won a prize in Columbia College's Video Festival, placing Silver in the dramatic video category. Looking back on it now, I think it was my tribute to my favorite Saturday morning show as a kid, Saved by the Bell.

Producing all these shows wasn't easy. I had to adapt the equipment creatively to keep an eye on the entire production. That meant having external monitors plugged into the camera so I could see what the camera operator was seeing, and lowering the editing devices to my level so that

I could piece together each show. I couldn't have done any of it without the help of my father, who came over after school practically every day to help me film the episodes.

During this time I also held the office of student government vice president. Taking charge came naturally. In order to do things other people could do on their own, however, I had to ask others for help. I couldn't afford the luxury of being shy. I realized I had to communicate my requests clearly and with confidence so that people could see I meant business. This was a skill I would come to rely on as the years went by.

"My Buddy Bill"

The only real cloud that appeared in high school was losing the election for student body president, something I had worked toward during my whole high school career. But I guess everything happens for a reason. Had I been elected president, I would never have been able to attend a program called Boys State, which ultimately led me to much greater opportunities.

Boys State, sponsored by the American Legion, was a gathering of boys from all over Illinois who were leaders in their schools. Out of one thousand boys in attendance, I worked my way up the ladder and got elected to the highest office, governor. This opened my life up to the national program, Boys Nation. Only ninety-six boys out of thirty-eight thousand in the United States are selected to attend this elite program. Boys Nation was attended by some of the truly best and brightest young men in the country. Alumni include three U.S. senators, four state governors, Pulitzer Prize–winner and movie critic Roger Ebert, and President William Jefferson Clinton. I was proud to be part of it.

I'll never forget the day my Boys Nation class spent five hours with President Clinton in the White House East Room. I wheeled up to him in the photo line.

The president gave me his thousand-watt smile and looked me right in the eye. "So, Sean, where are you from?"

"Chicago."

"Really? Well that's where Hillary is from. Actually, Sean, that's where the Democratic National Convention is being held this year."

"Well, Mr. President," I replied, "why don't you look me up when you're in town?"

Everyone laughed, even the serious Secret Service agents. Except I wasn't kidding. And sure enough, a few months later the president did look me up. During his campaign tour, he spotted me in a crowd of forty thousand individuals. He had the Secret Service pull me out of this sea of people, and he spent time with me behind the stage. Then he invited my family and me to sit in his presidential skybox at the United Center Stadium, where the Democratic National Convention was being held.

The night of convention, I waited in line as they checked us through security. One Chicago police officer asked me what I was doing at the convention. I told him the truth:

"I'm friends with the president."

He laughed at me, patted my head, and said condescendingly, "Sure you are, kid."

That night, I appeared live around the world on CNN. I didn't know that I was being filmed until after it was over. Apparently, during the president's speech, he made reference to Americans with disabilities, and they flashed a shot of me sitting proudly in his skybox. As I was leaving the stadium, I winked at the officer, who had just seen me on television. He laughed, this time at himself.

Developing Skills

If I could line up everyone who has doubted me, said I would never make it, and counted me out in life, the crowd would surely wrap to the moon and back.

So many people said, "Sure he's a nice, hard-working guy, BUT . . ."

That's all right. I hold no animosity toward them. It's more fun to be the underdog anyway—it makes for much better stories.

Politics took a front-row seat in my life for the next five years. I majored in political science in college, worked on a half-dozen campaigns, and earned prestigious internships, working on Capitol Hill for my U.S. congressman, William O. Lipinski, and ultimately in the White House alongside President Clinton.

My job in the White House was for the Office of Cabinet Affairs. My superior, Thurgood Marshall Jr., was the son of former Supreme Court Justice Thurgood Marshall and had himself won many legal accolades. I worked long hours, often putting in twelve-hour days. That summer, President Clinton was being investigated by Ken Starr, two U.S. Guards were shot and killed in the Capitol, drought fires spread across most of Florida, and U.S. embassies in Africa were bombed. There was never a dull moment— something I can also say about my life in general.

Never Count Yourself Out

Never count yourself out, even if the experts tell you that you don't stand a prayer. In 2001, I graduated from DePaul University in Chicago.

"Graduating with high honors, Sean Clinch Stephenson."

When my name was called, the packed auditorium burst into a three-minute ovation. The crowd was actually so loud they had to stop the processional for a few minutes. As I wheeled across the stage, I held my diploma up so high I felt as if I nearly scraped the ceiling. My parents wept with joy. Never in a million years would they have guessed that their frail little baby boy would go on to attend college right across the street from the very hospital in which doctors had predicted he would die soon after birth.

I was a college graduate, and I had my pick of jobs in the political sector. I had spent my entire academic career grooming myself to roll into a position in the legislative branch, yet I haven't set a wheel back in the political arena since I graduated. Destiny had other plans for me. John Lennon was so right when he said, "Life is what happens when you're busy making other plans."

Launching My Surprising Career

My surprise career choice snuck up on me when I least expected it. All through high school and college, I'd been asked to give speeches to companies, schools, and churches about how to overcome obstacles at home, in relationships, and at work. It brought in a little money here and there, just enough to support my habit of buying clothes, music, and video games, but it never struck me as a viable option for full-time work.

Then my dad sat me down. He said, "Sean, if your goal is to change the world, you could easily do that as a professional speaker. People love to listen to your stories, and they look up to you. Look at the impact a guy like Tony Robbins has made on the planet as a speaker."

He was right. The reason I loved politics was because it appeared to be an outlet that I could pursue to change the world. But professional speaking was an outlet too.

There was only one problem—I didn't know if I wanted to be a speaker. Did I really want to travel the country saying the same thing over and over for years?

As I wavered back and forth, my phone kept ringing with speaking opportunities. Finally, I took it as a sign. I needed to trust the universe and follow its lead. I began booking more speeches and honing my craft.

Back to School

I've been asked numerous times, "Sean, do you ever get nervous speaking on stage?"

The answer's simple. "No."

The act of speaking to people comes easily to me, and is quite enjoyable. When I started, though, I used to get nervous after my presentations when students would come up to me and ask for advice on the tough stuff.

"Sean, I think my friend is cutting herself. What should I do?"

"Sean, I'm afraid to tell my parents I'm gay. They're super religious, and I'm afraid they'll kick me out of the family. What should I do?"

"Sean, I think my dad is suicidal. I want to get him help. What should I do?"

Like I said, the tough stuff. I soon realized that I was in over my head.

I came to understand that motivating people for an hour on stage was not enough. I wanted to help the people in my audience develop a life that was free of inner strife and outer chaos. Inspiring quotes, colorful stories, and lighthearted activities weren't enough to bring about change on a deeper level. I felt ill-prepared to address the hurt of those who embraced me in tears after my talks.

So I dusted off my backpack and did something I thought I'd never do again. I went back to school. In August 2001, I enrolled in classes at Bennett/Stellar Academy and later at American Pacific University. I spent a combined total of three years in those schools, and received board certification in psychotherapy and neuro-linguistic programming from both institutions. And I wasn't finished then, either. On March 19, 2004, I enrolled in a PhD program in clinical hypnosis from American Pacific University. And just to make things really fun, at the same time I opened an office for the private practice in psychotherapy.

My Work as a Therapist

As soon as I opened up my private practice, people started coming to see me from far and wide to work on their issues. By September 2006, I had so many clients I had to move my practice into a larger location, a gorgeous skyscraper in Oakbrook Terrace, Illinois. My clients hear about me from all different sources: word of mouth, radio, TV, print media appearances, and my live speaking engagements. Some of my clients' stories would break your heart, make your stomach churn, and have you shaking your head in disbelief.

I've been told that I am different from any other therapist. I don't know if that's true, but maybe it's because I hold no judgments about those who've made ineffective choices in life. More likely, it's because clients take one look at me and think, "Hey, this guy has had troubles of his own. If he can make it, so can I!"

I *never* claim to know what they're going through—in fact, I can't stand that phrase, "I know what you're going through." *No one* can ever really know what another person is experiencing. I always tell my clients, "I don't have a clue what you're going through! I didn't grow up in your family, attend your school, have your set of past experiences, or live in your body. I'm really only an expert on one thing, and that's being me."

I guess you could say I'm an optimistic realist. As crass as it may sound, sometimes life does suck! Our challenge is to pull through and trust that we can alter the future with each choice we make in the present.

My Love Life

When I was twenty-four, I fell for a woman who had everything I was looking for. She was smart, attractive, and into physical fitness and spirituality, and had a really great head on her shoulders. We hit it off so well. Each time we went out, we got closer and closer, until we had "the talk."

"Sean, you're everything I'm looking for in a man, BUT . . ."

By now, you can guess the end of this sentence.

". . . I never wanted to spend my life with a little man in a wheelchair."

I hit rock bottom, swearing I never wanted to hear that statement ever again! That evening, I *knew* I would never be desired sexually and would remain single forever. I was convinced that the reason this curse was upon me was because of my physical disability, and I had plenty of evidence to prove it. I thought that women only wanted to date Mr. Tall, Dark, and Handsome.

No! I couldn't accept that I was banned for life from having a mate. So I did what I do best: I went out and learned everything I could about what women really want in a man. It would take four years.

I studied under some of the brightest minds in the field of sexual attraction and dating—Eben Pagan (who writes as David DeAngelo), Eric Von Sydow (who writes as Hypnotica), Adam Gilad (who writes as Grant Adams), Zan Perrion, Dr. Paul Dobransky, Dr. Amir Georges Sabongui, David Wygant, Lance Mason, Travis Decker, Neil Strauss (who writes as Style), and Owen Cook (who writes as Tyler Durden). What I found set my heart free.

Women don't want a man to *look* a certain way. They want a man to make them *feel* a certain way.

I flushed out my insecurities about looking different, being single, and not having much romantic experience for my age. I began to mature into a patient man who was secure in his own skin. I embraced the realization that I didn't need a woman on my arm to feel validated by others.

This caused a positive shift in my dating life. I began attracting and dating women who loved and accepted all of me. Eventually, I got so comfortable at attracting women that other men started to take notice. Men from across the globe began seeking me out for dating advice. They started flying in from all around the world to work with me on the issue of relationships with women in their own lives.

Eliminating the BUT

I wish I could go back in time, put my arm around that little boy crying alone in a biology lab, and tell him that one day he'd be attracting some of the most beautiful, talented, and loving women on the planet. Unfortunately, he probably wouldn't believe me. He had way too many BUTS.

I've learned that when people hide behind their limitations, they can't see anything else. That's why I have been on an endless pursuit to help wake people up—shake them if I have to, just to prove to them that they are capable of overcoming anything that might arise in their life. Sadly, it's sometimes nearly impossible to fight the greatest negative force on the planet: the size of one's BUT!

I have traveled to forty-seven states and six countries, meeting thousands of people a year. And here's what I've learned: *the only thing that has ever held you back from having what you want in life is the size of your BUT.*

Our BUT is that cushy excuse that we rest on when we want to quit, when we believe that there's nothing more we can do to resolve our challenges or accomplish our goals or fix our mistakes. Does any of this sound familiar?

Sure, I'd like to change, BUT . . .

- I'm too old/too young
- I'm too short/too tall
- I'm too fat/too skinny
- I'm not pretty/handsome enough
- I'm not smart enough
- I'm from a broken home
- I have a learning disability

Our BUTS are *huge*. And the longer we sit on them, the more they continue to grow! Here are just three examples that people who are stuck on their BUTS have shared with me over the years:

"I'd exercise and eat right, BUT I just don't have the time."

"I'd quit smoking, BUT I'm too stressed out."

"I'd ask that girl out, BUT what if she rejects me?"

I could fill the remaining pages of this book with nothing but examples of people sitting on their BUTS. In fact, a person could literally spend his entire life on his BUT. And a lot of people do.

How Some Folks Can Keep You on Your BUT

It's sad to think that people are often pressured to stay on their BUTS by their own friends and family, but that's what often happens.

Why do some people feel the need to tear down others when they see progress being made? Short answer: we don't like to be left behind. If you get off your BUT while your friends are still sitting on theirs, they fear you might drift away from them. That feeling of separation is unnerving for most people. If you are getting better, then they must—in contrast—be worse. And no one likes to feel like that. They'd rather keep you on your BUT right alongside them.

Besides separation and humiliation, we humans don't like seeing those we love get hurt. People who love you don't want to see you try to get off your BUT only to end up "failing." Fear makes them keep you on your BUT.

Finally, and most likely, one of the biggest reasons people don't like to see their friends and family get off their BUT is that it's a huge reminder that maybe it's time for them to do the same. Self-reflection, when placed right in front of your face, can cause feelings of discomfort. That's why many alcoholics don't like to drink alone, food addicts want you to join them in dessert, and procrastinators want you to blow off your work and goof around with them.

Humans are funny creatures. We claim to want honesty, yet we are often in total denial. We lie to ourselves on a regular basis. We proclaim to the world that we want something, yet we won't put forth the effort to get it. Or we say that we don't mind our current condition, yet we secretly hate it. We hate being financially strapped, overweight, lonely, or controlled; we hate feeling emotionally or physically inhibited. Habit convinces us that it's much easier to act as if everything were fine the way it is than to actually do something to change things.

Nope. Not true! You really *can* get off your BUTS. And it's not as hard as that negative tape loop playing in your mind tells you it will be.

Why We Sit on Our BUTS

Most people sit on their BUTS for one of three reasons.

1. They truly believe that their BUT is holding them back. They literally can't move.
2. Getting off their BUT is too big a risk. It's easier to be in the unhappy state they're used to than to take the chance to be happy. The thinking goes like this: you know that if you don't study for the test, you are more than likely to fail it; yet if you study hard, you still aren't guaranteed an A. Some people would rather stay stuck on their BUTS, addicted to the certainty of failure, than risk the possibility of disappointment.

3. They're mired in a mixture of reasons 1 and 2. They're partially hypnotized into believing that their BUT will forever hold them back, plus they find it easier to keep the status quo than to see what would happen if they tried to change it.

You know what? None of this is true. The sad truth is, the more you sit on your BUT, the weaker you get. If you never use your muscles, they eventually atrophy. The longer you stay frozen in that place of fear, excuses, or insecurity, the harder it becomes to get up off it. As long as you're stuck on your BUT, you'll never go after what you really want in life.

You may be able to see what you want, but it will always be just out of reach.

Is that really what you want?

I didn't think so!

Get Off Your BUT Now!

This book is organized into six lessons designed to help you get off your BUT. Please read them in order: I've arranged them this way to give you a great foundation! Each lesson includes activities, and to get the most from the lessons, I encourage you to give these activities your full attention. You will need what I call a Get Off Your BUT Now! journal for your written responses, and it can be as fancy or as simple as you like. Following each of Lessons 1 through

5, you'll read inspiring true stories about how friends of mine got off their BUTS to overcome challenging circumstances. Avoid the temptation to skip over these stories for the sake of saving time. They are extremely entertaining, not to mention critical to ending self-sabotage for good. Of course, in each lesson you'll continue to learn more about me and my friends, and—most important—you'll learn more about yourself, what has been holding you back from living your life to the fullest, and the wonderful places you can go when you get off your BUT.

My life has been one of a kind. I was born with certain challenges and certain gifts, blessed with parents who supported me totally, and given some great opportunities. You too were born with challenges and gifts, talents and opportunities. I hope you'll take *this* opportunity to start believing in yourself. Because no matter how big your BUT is, or how long you've been sitting on it, together—right now, in the chapters of this book—we are going to work on creating a life that is more exciting and fulfilling than you ever dreamed possible.

Ready?

Let's get started.

LESSON 1

Start Connecting

The bus driver was about fifty-five, balding, and overweight, with a sad, sweet smile. "Call me Boston Bill," he said as I boarded his bus.

It was a little past 10:00 PM. My family and I were completely exhausted. Bad weather had caused our flight home to be canceled, and even though we'd waited standby at the airport all day, we'd had no luck. Our only choice was to stay in Boston overnight. Needless to say, we were not too chipper as we climbed into Bill's hotel shuttle. Worse, the little bus was not wheelchair accessible, so I had to be strapped into a child's car seat, riding shotgun next to Bill. I was a very tired ten-year-old who just wanted to go to sleep, but Bill seemed nice. I brushed off my bad day and turned on my good vibes.

We talked the whole ride, from the airport to the hotel. The time went by easily as I joked around with Bill, asking him a million and one questions. When we finally arrived, I said my good-byes and wished him well.

It was late, but my family and I were famished. We headed for the hotel dining room for a quick meal. The restaurant was closing down as we walked in, but the hostess took pity on us. I'm guessing we looked too hungry and worn out to turn away. When the food came, I dug in.

About halfway through my pasta marinara, I looked up to see Bill making a beeline to our table. He wasn't smiling now, though. Instead, he had that expression all humans make right before they cry.

"I hope you don't mind that I'm interrupting your dinner," he said to my parents. "I just had to share something with you." He placed his hand gently on the top of my head.

"I've been going through a rough period in my life lately," he continued. "My wife left me, my kids won't speak to me, and I've been drinking too much. I've been going to therapists and counselors, but none of them were able to get through to me. Before this little guy here got on my bus, I was seriously considering committing suicide tonight." By this time, we'd all put down our forks and were listening intently.

"But your son here did more for me in a short trip from the airport than all the therapists combined. After meeting this boy, and seeing how happy he is despite everything that he has to deal with, well, it put my life in perspective. I have hope now, and I just wanted to thank you."

Crying quietly, he kissed the top of my head and walked away before we could say anything. Mom, Dad, Heidi, and I just sat there in silence, as though we'd witnessed some kind of miracle. I was mystified.

I thought, *What did I do?* I just sat on his bus and asked him questions about himself and teased him a little. I was just trying to be a nice person. I didn't burst into a burning building and risk my life to save him or anything.

This experience puzzled me for years. Then one day, when I was in my early twenties, I was sitting in a seminar listening to a highly regarded professional speaker. He was sharing great information, and he was obviously very intelligent. Nevertheless, the audience was restless, fidgeting, and bored—a woman sitting near me had actually fallen asleep. It was painfully obvious that no one was able to pay attention. I knew that the information he wanted to communicate was valuable, so why didn't anyone feel compelled to listen?

Suddenly, it came to me! He simply lacked the one component that must exist in order for one human being to feel emotionally moved, inspired, and safe with another human being: the ability to make a connection. I made an earthshaking distinction: *communication is merely an exchange of information, but connection is an exchange of our humanity.*

And right then and there, I flashed back to my bus ride with Boston Bill. Now it all made sense. Now I could see why what I had thought was just conversation had changed Bill's life. I was paying attention to him, listening to him, teasing and joking and having fun with him. *I had established a deep connection with him*, a connection that apparently no one else had made with him during all his years of "communicating."

Now, sitting in the audience, I realized the speech was over. Everyone stood up and filed out of the auditorium quietly; there was not a trace of happiness or warmth on people's faces. Communication without connection had actually drained them of energy!

In that moment, I decided to set out on a quest to find out what the experience of connection was all about. Along the way, I learned that we can talk to others and ourselves all we want, and never get anywhere. It's the act of truly connecting—not only with other human beings but with yourself—that is step one in getting yourself off your BUT.

Remember, we're all in this together!

Why Should We Have to Connect?

Imagine if I had said to myself, "I *could* interact with Boston Bill, BUT . . . I'm too tired, and it's not going to do me any good!" The imagined outcome of that decision makes me shudder. The BUTS that hold us back from connecting with our fellow earthlings keep our souls in the dark. I truly believe that our major social ills would disappear if we just spent our lives perfecting the art of connecting with each other.

Why? Because it's *impossible* to do harm to anyone with whom we feel truly connected. Malice cannot coexist with connection. Even if we try to entertain the thought of hurting someone we're truly connected with, we immediately recoil, horrified at the mere idea.

BUT . . . people hurt the ones they love all the time! How can they do this? Simple: their connection with the person is somehow broken. As long as we remain connected—really connected—we're not going to do deliberate harm to our loved ones, friends, family, colleagues, and clients. It's simply not possible.

So what *is* connection, anyway?

How We Can Tell When We're Connected

Connection comes into being the moment that one individual feels that another genuinely cares about him or her. As soon as this genuine caring energy is mutually experienced, the connection is reciprocated. Both parties know a connection has been created the instant it happens.

If you and I have a real connection, we'll be able to communicate on a deep level. But if I feel as if you don't care about me, even though you might have the best advice on the planet, I will feel zero interest in implementing your words of wisdom. And if a child, teenager, or college student doesn't feel that her teacher, coach, counselor, or assembly speaker really cares about her well-being—forget about it! All that good advice will just fall to the floor and blow away like dust.

By design, you are built to recognize who cares about you and who does not. It's hardwired in your biology for a very good reason. Eons of evolution have turned our brains into very effective danger detectors. If we feel that someone doesn't care about us, we also feel intuitively that he could do us harm. We want nothing to do with him, for our own good.

Connection Versus Communication

A student once asked me, "If connection is so valuable, why don't we integrate courses on it into our academic curriculum?"

Good question. Unfortunately, at this point, we're only teaching our future generations about how to communicate with each other.

Communication is valuable too. I would certainly be unable to share this idea of connection without the existence of communication! Clearly, if we were unable to exchange information through spoken and printed words, our early societies wouldn't have evolved into the complex, information-driven human civilization in which we live today.

However, without taking the next step in our evolution— from communication to connection—our society is going to have a million devices for staying in close communication, yet we will have no greater purpose motivating us to do so. We see it now, even in this very day and age. We have instant messaging, texting, e-mailing, faxing, cell phones . . . yet, if anything, we feel more isolated and lonelier than ever. I often wonder if our great-great ancestors felt more connected to each other than we do.

Emotional Energy Is the Fuel That Powers Connection

I'm a huge technology buff, always up on the latest phones and Internet services. I love these communication devices, yet I am quick to remember their purpose: to bring us closer together so that we can share our caring energy anytime and anywhere on the planet.

We need electricity to make our communication devices operate. What's the primary fuel that powers authentic human connection?

Emotion!

Every individual (barring neurological dysfunction) is capable of feeling emotions. We've all felt happy, sad, lonely, excited, confused, afraid . . . The spectrum of human emotion is vast and rich. I can't ever know exactly what you're going through in life, but I do know that you and I have both experienced similar emotions.

Without emotion, life would be nothing more than a series of mechanical maneuvers. The movie Equilibrium provides a glimpse of what society might look like if human emotion were removed: violence would be eradicated with the elimination of aggression, but because passion and expression would also be gone, art, comedy, and music would not exist.

I don't want to live in that sort of world. Do you?

Ten Things I Learned About Connection from President Bill Clinton

Love him or loathe him, you can't deny that Bill Clinton is a masterful connection artist. I've seen him in action many times, and he's a wonder to behold. How does he do it? How can he connect with people who despise him, and within a few minutes have them laughing, hugging, and listening closely to him?

During the time I worked for the president as a White House intern, I watched him closely, trying to figure out his secret. The first thing I noticed was that he always paid very close attention to how other people were feeling. If they retreated emotionally during an exchange, he immediately reengaged them and brought them back on course. He had an infinite number of techniques, but these were the ones I saw him use most often:

1. **He told a story.** This was far less intrusive—and way more effective—than making his point directly. And his story would always evoke specific emotions from the listeners—laughter, anger, compassion—that would help them connect with what he was communicating.

2. **He made physical contact.** On many occasions, he would place his hand on your shoulder, back, or forearm as he spoke, passing his energy on to you kinetically.

3. **He remembered your name.** This one baffled and amazed me. The number of people a president meets in the course of one year in office is overwhelming. He couldn't possibly remember them all. Yet if Clinton met you on more than a few occasions, he would retain your name perfectly and use it every time he spoke to you. Which brings us to the next point.

4. **He called you by name.** Whether he remembered it or had to glance down quickly at your name badge, he would make sure to call you by name more than once in the course of his conversation with you. During one of the recent post-term visits I had with him, he walked into the room and said warmly, "Sean, boy am I glad to see you." Someone once told me that the sound of our own name spoken in a loving tone is one of the most soothing sounds we can ever hear. I agree.

5. **He made deep eye contact with you.** Once President Clinton's eyes locked onto yours, they didn't leave until the interaction was complete. In all my years of talking to celebrities, from sports icons and Hollywood starlets to business moguls and politicians, few have used this technique with such finesse. Most of these ego-monsters can't hold the connection more than a few seconds before they start scanning

the room for someone more important to talk to than the person right in front of them. Yuck!

6. **He used his facial expressions to convey his emotional state.** President Clinton would greet you with a smile in his eyes on a joyous occasion, and with sad eyes and an expression of empathy in moments of devastation. If he was upset about something, it showed on his face like a summer storm. I'm sure there were times, as there are for all of us, when he felt one emotion and projected another. But he never seemed false around me—he was always successful in conveying the emotion he wanted to show.

7. **He calibrated his vocal inflections and volume based on the amount of rapport he had established.** If the rapport was strong, he would be more boisterous in his volume. If it was weak, he would have a more soft-spoken demeanor. Simple, but effective.

8. **He asked for your opinion.** The first time the president turned to me and asked, "Sean, what are your thoughts on that?" I thought, "Did he just ask *me* for my opinion?" Whether he asked because he really wanted to know or because he knew it was tremendously flattering to be asked a question by the leader of the free world, I'm not exactly sure. I do know that it felt good, and I remember it to this day. Humans love to give their opinions on things. On those rare occasions when we are actually asked our thoughts on

something—and we are listened to—it makes us feel tremendously important.

9. **He chose his words wisely.** Never once did I catch
President Clinton taking the verbal low road, slinging slang
with disregard. He carefully selected every word to create
just the right expression he was looking for.

10. **He praised you publicly any chance he got.** On
July 24, 1998, I was attending an event in the Rose Garden,
when out of the blue the president said, "I'd also like to
thank Sean Stephenson, [Boys Nation] class of 1996, now
an intern in Cabinet Affairs. Thank you for what you are
doing here." Then he nodded and smiled in my direction.
Was he doing that because it was standard protocol, or
because he really was truly grateful for my service at the
White House? I'm going to choose to believe the latter. It
felt great.

Sometimes I affectionately refer to President Clinton's
gift of connecting to those who don't like him as "the
carwash phenomenon." Dignitaries and their families—
specifically the ones who were skeptical and unfriendly
toward him—would enter the White House through the
East Wing gates, often with expressions of disdain. They
would take a tour of all the public areas and then work
their way over to the president's office in the West Wing,
to meet with him. A few hours later, when they exited the

White House through the West Wing gates, they looked completely different. It was as if President Clinton, like a cosmic car wash, had magically washed away their scowls and replaced them with expressions of pure relaxation. Absolutely remarkable!

It's been said that Clinton's greatest skill is his ability to communicate. I would disagree. I believe his strongest suit is being able to connect.

What If You Feel Too Shy to Connect?

More than one client has said to me, "I get that connection is important, Sean, BUT . . . I'm just too shy."

No one would ever call me shy, but I know that individuals fall on a spectrum from extreme introverts to extreme extroverts. But no matter what our personal style, sometimes we just identify ourselves as "shy." Why?

"Shy" behavior exists for many reasons. The greatest is that *we think* it keeps us from getting hurt. If we don't get involved, we can't fail, be made fun of, disappoint someone else, or look bad in any way. I call this the "turtle complex." If I curl up and hide in my shell, you can't get to me . . . Meanwhile, though, I'm missing out on the juice of life: *connection!*

Shy behavior is triggered the second we start thinking about ourselves. The moment we start thinking and acting selflessly, reaching out to help those around us, shyness subsides.

GET OFF YOUR BUT *NOW!*
Getting from Shy to Fly

Opportunities to connect with others are available to us every day—in the coffee shop, at the watercooler, and in the line at the bank. Too many people never capitalize on these opportunities because they have identified with the behavior of shyness, creating a strong barrier to connection. Guess what the antidote to shyness is?

Connecting!

Next time you're out and about, try this and see what happens:

First, just pretend you're *not* shy. Ask the person behind the cash register at the store how her day was, and don't stop at "Fine." Listen to what she tells you, and get curious about the little details. Ask her follow-up questions, such as

"What do you love about your job?"
"If you could have any job in the world, what would you want to do?"
"What are you looking forward to tomorrow?"

Pay attention to how you feel before you start talking—you'll probably be a bit nervous!—and be sure to pay attention to how you feel at the end of the conversation.

Then do it again!

We're All Connected

Connection is not just about being friendly; it's about actually recognizing that the person you're interacting with is going through his own set of problems and pain, just like yourself. It's so easy to wander through life acting as if everyone around you were a hologram, not really there, separate from you. This is *so* not true.

We are all connected. When we remember that, we can see ourselves in the eyes of others—and others in ourselves. Every form of religion and science that I've ever studied always comes back to this very point: we're all connected.

Why I Love Everyone

Here's what one client said to me during a therapy session:

"I'd like to connect with everyone, BUT . . . some people are just jerks. I refuse to be nice to them."

Connecting with people you like is not much of a feat. It's easy to connect with someone who praises you, showers you with positive attention, and wants to see you succeed. This is good practice, especially if connections are one of your biggest BUTS. But you'll build the real skill of connection by connecting with people who annoy and frustrate you.

I'm not saying you have to be friends with these people, but don't make the mistake of thinking that connection should be reserved for your personal fan club. We need to connect with *everyone* in order to truly connect with ourselves.

In fact, I've stated many times that I love *everyone!*

What? How can I make such a blanket statement?

Simply put, I love everyone so that no one can own me. If I hate another person, she owns me. It's true. Watch what happens in your life when you don't like someone:

- He owns your very thoughts, every time you think about how awful he is.
- He owns the conversations you have when you complain about him to your friends.
- He even owns your behavior, when you change your plans to avoid him.

When we hate someone, we become her little marionette. She can make us bob up and down, side to side, in any direction she chooses—that is, until we finally stop hating her and move on. Not being controlled by another person is not the only reason for loving everyone, but it is certainly a very important motivator.

Connecting Is Great—Even When It Hurts!

I learned the power of connecting to difficult people when I was in college, taking a child psychology course. I was assigned to an elementary school several miles from my campus. My project consisted of working with a group of forty kids, ranging from kindergartners to sixth graders. These children were in a special program designed for children from families with two working parents or with single parents who had to work and needed to drop their children off a few hours before school started and pick them up a few hours after school ended.

One afternoon, I had them all in the school gymnasium, sitting in a semicircle around me at half-court. I was teaching them valuable life lessons—the importance of loving yourself, being kind to your classmates, why it's important to share . . . and then a shoe came flying out of nowhere and hit me squarely on my left temple.

Ow!

I was pretty certain that shoes don't fly by themselves, and sure enough I saw a one-shoed boy sitting in the circle, laughing hysterically at his obnoxious prank.

What would be the normal, instinctive thing to do in a case like this, with the pain of a heavy gym shoe burning in the middle of a red spot on the side of your head? Throw it back? I wanted to. But I was supposed to be a responsible teacher in a public classroom. Should I take the child out in the hall and have some choice words with him? Sure, that would have been a good idea. But for whatever reason—shock, pain, inexperience, immaturity—I did absolutely nothing. In fact, I went so far as to pretend it didn't happen. Thankful the shoe hadn't caused me lasting damage, I just went on trying to connect with the kids around me, including the boy I was now thinking of as the Shoeless Monster.

Eventually, the day ended. The kids were picked up by their parents one by one until I was left with one child. Guess who? Yep, the Shoeless Monster. We sat there for forty-five minutes, my head still smarting, just talking. I was still mad at him—what kind of kid throws a shoe at his teacher?

Finally, the door swung open, and an older woman walked slowly into the gym.

"It's time to go," she said, grabbing the boy by the hand.

"See you later, Mr. Sean!" he said, with glee in his voice. He seemed to like me.

"Can't wait!" I said, giving him the smile adults make when they know the child is too young to understand sarcasm.

I collected my stuff and headed to my vehicle, glad to be leaving the Shoeless Monster and the day behind. I was half-way there when I heard a booming voice. "Sean, wait up!"

It was the school principal.

"Sean," he said, "how's your project coming? How are all the kids?"

"They're all a bunch of angels, except for this one child!" Then I told him the shoe story.

"I know just the boy you're talking about," he said. "You need to know something about this kid."

"I already know he's quite a pain!" I said, rubbing my head.

"Well, Sean, what you don't know is that just about a year ago this boy's father killed his mother . . . and now his father is in prison, and the only living relative around to take care of him is his grandmother. She had to pick up two side jobs just to support the two of them. For lunch, he often comes to school with just a candy bar and a soda. He doesn't get much attention at home. I just thought you should know this."

Now all I wanted was to give this kid a huge hug and become a loving mentor in his life. I'm so glad I didn't throw the shoe back; that wouldn't have solved anything.

That day taught me more about life than the rest of all my collegiate experience combined: people are not their behavior; there is never any use in throwing the shoe back.

We often get so caught up in our lives that when someone comes along and disturbs us or makes things difficult, we think, "How dare you interrupt my life!" Rarely do we ever have the full picture. Even if we think we know someone, and understand what she is going through, we actually don't. *We can't.* We are not living in her skin.

The Shoeless Monster's behavior was not condonable, but it was certainly forgivable. We must look past people's behavior and ask what's going on in their inner world that's causing brash, rude, selfish, and hurtful actions in their outer world. Again: people are not their behavior.

I love the part in the movie *Peaceful Warrior* when the main character says, "The ones who are the hardest to love are usually the ones who need it most." I couldn't agree more. When we've been hurt, all we know how to do is hurt others. As soon as we heal ourselves, we are able to heal others.

This little boy was hurt, and he was crying out for help using the best method his little mind could conjure up. It was as if he were trying to get my attention, to signal to me, "Sean, please walk a mile in my shoe . . . I need your help!"

GET OFF YOUR BUT *NOW!*
Taming the Shoeless Monster

Can you tame your own Shoeless Monsters? You might be able to, if you remember this important fact: your goal is not to correct their behavior; it's to help them out of the bear trap their mind and heart are stuck in. This won't be easy, but it certainly will be worth it.

1. **Make a list.** In your Get Off Your BUT Now! journal, write down the names of all the people you have to deal with regularly who are annoying, selfish, rude, or obnoxious, or who exhibit any other destructive behaviors.

2. **Take an honest look.** To what extent are you simply being judgmental? Are you quite possibly projecting your issues onto them when they might have no issue at all? If that's not the case and you are really sure that your Shoeless Monster(s) is destructive, go on to step 3.

3. **Discover what's behind their behavior.** This isn't a license for you to pry into their private business or to tell them that their behavior sucks. It *is* a license for you to show them that you care about them. Help them understand that you have no clue as to what they're going through, but that if they ever need to talk, you'll be there for them with no judgment.

Connecting with Some Really Tough Customers

The first time I spoke at a maximum security prison, my friends asked me, "Were you scared?"

To be honest, I was more scared of the prison than the prisoners. Once I got past all the razor-sharp fences, armed guards, and heavy metal gates, all I could see was a group of men—not prisoners or criminals, but men. Many of them were my age or younger. Sure, these men had made poor choices—extremely poor choices. But I knew that if I wanted to be a part of their "correction," it was up to me to see them as humans, no less than I.

So the first words out of my mouth were, "I just want you to know that I respect you." That got their attention. I could tell that this group of individuals hadn't been given respect without having to beat it out of someone.

"You know," I continued, "we have something in common." That really got their attention.

"I'm imprisoned by my physical condition, and you're imprisoned by your past. I think we can learn a lot from each other."

Commonality, I knew, is imperative for connection, and I could see that they agreed with my statement—many of them leaned forward and began listening to me as if I had the secrets to the universe. As my speech progressed, they began nodding in agreement with me, little smiles began replacing their guarded looks, and I knew we had forged a connection.

If real connection can take place between a tiny guy in a wheelchair who's never even shoplifted a candy bar, and physically intimidating men whose rap sheets are a mile long, then anyone can make a connection with anyone else.

You can too.

How? By finding your commonalities.

We like people who are like us. We feel disconnected from anyone whose life seems drastically different from ours. Looks, money, age, race, religion, intelligence, education . . . these are all elements that can make us feel different from others. So if we want to connect with an individual or a group of individuals, we must find a common thread—no matter how unlikely it seems.

It can be really simple:

"Did you see the game last night?"

"Can you believe the gas prices today?"

"What's with this weather?"

As soon as we find common ground, connection can take place.

GET OFF YOUR BUT *NOW!*
Vulnerability—The Glue of Connection

The most effective way to find common ground is by sharing our vulnerabilities. As hard as we work at maintaining an appearance of "having it all together," we actually connect best in those moments when we admit we don't.

Trying to appear perfect and superior kills connection. Think about it. When was the last time you heard someone talk on and on about his accomplishments and strengths and you ended up feeling closer to him? Never. We bond through our imperfections and shortcomings. Authenticity and vulnerability are the glue of connection. So let's make some glue, shall we?

1. In your journal, make a list of ten things that are slightly embarrassing about yourself that *no one* would ever guess about you—the more ironic the better. Here are some examples:

    "Even though I'm an accountant, I have to use a calculator for basic math."
    "I'm a nutritional coach, yet sometimes I crave Spam and Cheetos."
    "I'm an author, but I don't like to read."

2. When appropriate—at a dinner party, not a job interview!—share some of the items from your list. These insights into your authentic self are pure gold to share with people whom you want to connect with; they show that you're not pretending to be someone you're not.

3. When you find yourself in a group of disparate individuals, you can bring the group together by doing a little detective work to find out what everyone has in common. Share your own interests—you'll be surprised how quickly the group relaxes and connections start forming!

Connecting Through Conversational Ping-Pong

Have you ever been in a conversation with someone who was painfully boring and seemed to drone on forever? You were probably looking at your watch, frantically trying to figure out how to get away. Obviously, there was no connection present. Moments of strong connection, in contrast, are so pleasurable that we lose all track of time.

So how do we spark connection in a conversation? We have to play Ping-Pong.

Huh?

Ping-Pong works like this: you take a ball and serve it back and forth on a table, over a net. What would happen if you hit the ball across the net and the other player never hit it back? Or if the person serving the ball just held on to it and never hit it over to you? How fun would that be? Yet that's how many of us converse with others. Either we hog the ball and just talk about our lives the whole time, or we never play at all.

If you want to master the art of connection through conversation, just remember to play verbal Ping-Pong. I love to talk, so I have to check in with myself all the time: "Sean . . . has the ball been on their side of the table much during this conversation?" If the answer is no, I quickly say that I've been going on about myself, but I really want to catch up on what's happening with them. You can't fake it, though. Talking for an hour straight about your life and ending with, "Gotta go—by the way, how are you?" is not going to cut it! Neither is asking them a bunch of questions about their life but not sharing anything about yourself. In order for people to feel connected to you, they need to know how you're doing, what you're up to, and how you've been feeling. If you hide behind a battery of questions, a person may feel as if you care about him, but he will have nothing invested in you.

Once you've mastered conversational Ping-Pong, you can take it to the next level. At the beginning of a conversation, recall and mention some of the things the person told you in your last interaction. "What happened with that

car you were talking about buying the last time we spoke?"
This tells her that you care enough about her to remember
and be interested in what she has to say.

Women are pretty good at this. Unfortunately, most
men really fall down on the job on this one. How powerful
is the man (or woman) who can see a person three weeks
later and ask,

"What outfit did you end up wearing to that party you told
    me about?"

"Did they ever find your camera?"

"So did the blind date work out?"

When your friend is flattered and touched that you
remembered, and hits the ball back to your side of the
table, the connection will be made.

There's Always Time for Connection

I often hear people say, "I'd do all this connection stuff,
BUT . . . I'm just too busy."

We all fall prey to the idea that we don't have enough
time. Yet time is the only commodity that we've all been
given an equal amount of.

The excuse of "not having time" is never really
about time; it's about priorities. If you don't set making

connections as a high priority, you'll never feel that there's time for it. Ironically, when you don't spend a little extra time connecting with your friends, family, lovers, and colleagues, you'll end up spending tons of time on the back end repairing hurt feelings and enduring endless amounts of drama.

If you set the goal of authentically connecting for *just a few minutes a day*, you'll be amazed at the positive reactions you get. Romantic dates, free meals, pay raises, party invitations . . . connecting is giving, and people always want to give back. Can you really afford the time *not* to connect?

Recently, at the airport, I overheard two friends talking. One of the guys said that he really liked this girl who worked at his office, but he never let her know. Years went by, but he never reached out to her, never made any effort to connect with her on a personal level. Then one day she showed up at work with a huge rock on the fourth finger of her left hand. When she showed him, he said, "That's great" in a somewhat sarcastic tone. Then he walked away.

His reaction upset her so much that she asked around the office, trying to understand why he wasn't happy for her. Surprised, her colleagues told her that it was obvious that he had always had a crush on her. She collapsed in her chair, crying. "I've always had a crush on him too," she sobbed, "but I thought he didn't like me because he never talked to me . . . and now it's too late!" The man telling the story was crushed. At this point his friend reached over and patted him on the back.

We can't procrastinate when it comes to making connections. When we see the window of opportunity, we have
to reach out and connect—no BUTS about it. In fact, I believe
we put ourselves in real danger when we refuse to connect
with others. Like this man and woman, we can not only lose
positive opportunities but also incur negative consequences.

I've read that doctors who don't connect with their
patients on a personal level are far more prone to being
sued for malpractice—even if they didn't do anything
medically wrong. This is because the second a patient has a
pain or complication, he'll find it easier and more natural
to think that it must have been caused by the doctor who
didn't really care about him.

GET OFF YOUR BUT NOW!
Fun with Connecting

Connecting with others doesn't have to be elaborate or deeply meaningful or planned in advance. It
doesn't even have to result in a long-lasting relationship.
A quick connection with strangers can make both of
you feel great for the rest of the day and teach you one
of the most important lessons about connecting: it's fun!

1. **Make a silly face.** Make eye contact with the person
   you want to connect with, and then make a silly

face—simply to make her smile—and then smile to show your intent. Obviously, you'll want to keep this appropriate to the context! But given the right time, place, and person, you'll be amazed by how much you can brighten someone's day with a silly face—and how good it makes you feel in return.

2. **Make a hand sandwich.** Next time you're introduced to someone who reaches out to shake your hand, place *both* of your hands comfortably around his, making a nice hand sandwich. Look deep into his eyes, smile, nod, and say, "It's a pleasure to meet you." He will connect with your warmth as genuine, and it will be.

3. **Play "What I Love About You."** This is a great game to play on a road trip or when you're sitting around the dinner table with your friends, family, or a lover. Go around the group, taking turns saying what you love about each other and listening to what they love about you. I learned this one from a kindergarten teacher who had me speak to her class. We played the game for over thirty minutes, and I loved it so much that I adopted it into my life. I now play at least a few times a month—on dates, on the phone with friends, and on road trips with my family. (*Warning*: Never play "What I Can't Stand About You"! That one ends really badly for everyone . . . trust me, I know!)

4. **Play the Question Game.** This is a great game to play
   when you want to connect with someone and get to
   know her at the same time. The premise is simple:
   you take turns asking questions about each other. The
   more creative the questions, the more fun the game.
   For example, "What's something about you that no
   one would ever guess?" "If you could eliminate one
   negative thing on this planet, what would it be?"
   (*Warning:* This game is not Truth or Dare! Be nice.)

   I once played this game with a woman who
   answered the question, "What is a simple pleasure you love more than anything on earth?" Her
   answer was animal crackers. So the next time we got
   together, guess what I started nibbling on when she
   showed up. Priceless connection builder!

By now, I think you understand how passionate I am when
it comes to connection!

Connecting with others is never about appearing to
be perfect, and it's about much more than being nice or
polite. We make connections when we open up our authentic self and share the things that make us all human—the
good and the bad, warts and all. It's also about using genuine emotional tools like listening, focusing, and empathy

to step into the world of another human being as best you can, making both of your realities happier, safer, and more fulfilling. And there's a bonus: the more you connect with those around you, the more support you'll get from others.

In the next lesson, you'll learn how to improve the most important (yet often overlooked) connection you'll ever have: the connection you have with yourself.

HOW RENE GOT OFF HIS BUT

"I'd be successful, BUT I was born into poverty."

I was extremely impressed by Rene Godefroy the first day I ever saw him. He was on stage, sharing his life story with an audience of over two thousand professional speakers. Speaking to two thousand people is a feat unto itself; however, speaking to two thousand *speakers* is in a totally different league of intimidation! Yet he communicated his points with such grace and poise that I sat back in awe. I felt as if he were speaking directly to me. Considering the fact that English was not even his first language, I found Rene beyond amazing.

After his presentation, I rolled up to him and introduced myself. We hit it off immediately. He was as great at communicating one on one as he was to a group, yet I found that his communication skills actually paled in comparison to his connection skills. I felt that he was truly interested in getting to know me, that he was really listening and paying attention to what I had to say. He was both inquisitive and genuine, two attributes that ignite connection. How he handled himself on and off stage that day convinced me that I was in the presence of a man who had what it takes to connect with all of humanity. His life story says it all.

Rene was born in Haiti, in a tiny, impoverished village without running water, electricity, or medical care. When he was nine months old, his mother left him behind with a neighbor and went to Port-au-Prince to find a better way to provide for her son and, she hoped, break the cycle of poverty.

Right after Rene's mother left, he became very ill. Have you seen those infomercials about suffering children in third-world countries? That's how life was for Rene.

His diet consisted of breadfruit, a starchy food that tastes something like a potato. He ate it for breakfast, lunch, and dinner. But his weak digestive system simply could not process all the starch, and his tummy would swell.

Because his only source of water was from an untreated source, parasites grew inside of him. Those parasites were sucking the life out of him. Many nights he would be tormented with severe stomach cramps, crawling on the dirt floor in the dark calling for his mother, who was not around to help him.

Rene was so ill and frail that when the strong tropical winds blew across the village, he would run and brace himself against a tree so that he wouldn't get blown away. To add insult to injury, he was teased and ridiculed.

Finally, when Rene was seven, his mother was able to afford to send for him. Now you're probably thinking, "What a relief! No more misery for Rene." Wrong. Life in the city with his mother was just as bad. You see, Rene's mother lived in a little basement shack infested with rats and roaches.

At night, he slept on the floor on some ragged sheets, trying to ignore the critters that crawled over him. The rats terrified him, nibbling at the bottoms of his feet. Despite all his hardships, Rene grew up. Sometimes he dreamed about going to the United States, which he called the "promise land."

When he was eighteen, Rene sat on a small bench and watched a group of guys rehearsing for a play. He thought to himself, "I sure would love to perform with this group." His mind, however, had other ideas. It said, "BUT I don't have any experience or training."

Then one day, in spite of his fears, he decided to stop listening to his BUT. He walked right up to the man in charge of the group and asked if he could join—and, to his surprise, the answer was yes. I wasn't surprised when I heard this part of the story, though. I'm sure that Rene must have looked that man in the eye, connecting and communicating his heart's intention on the spot. How could the man have refused?

So, at the age of twenty-one, Rene left Haiti with a theatre company bound for Montreal, Canada. Once there, he inquired about the United States. When they told him that it was just next door, he couldn't believe it.

Right away, he began to ask everyone he met about the best way to get to America. Most people tried to discourage him. They told him how risky and dangerous it was. Many suggested that it was almost impossible. Then someone told him about a woman who was smuggling people into the United States.

"It's dangerous," the man said. "You might even get killed." Rene arrived in the United States wedged between the rear tires of a tractor trailer, flat on his elbows and knees. Trembling, terrified, covered with ashes, dust, and smoke, Rene made his prayer: "God, if you help me make it to America safe, I promise I will do something meaningful with my life."

And he did. He washed cars on the streets of Miami from 1983 to 1984, and mopped floors from 1984 to 1985. He worked as a doorman in Atlanta for fourteen years. Along the way he tried to communicate with everyone he met, and through those efforts he learned English—one word at a time. While parking cars for a living, he discovered self-help books lying on the backseats, and his curiosity was piqued. He reasoned, "If those rich people are reading those kinds of books, then I should read them, too. Maybe they know something I don't know."

He started buying more self-help books, devouring them from beginning to end. Through the books, he discovered that some of these authors were "motivational speakers." He was stunned to find out that such a career existed. He said to himself, "I want to be a motivational speaker in the United States of America."

Then a BUT appeared: "BUT my English is not good enough and my accent is too thick." Rene faced those BUTS

head-on and took the plunge in spite of them. He started
the journey to becoming a motivational speaker in North
America. Rene's grit, determination, and unwavering commitment helped him blast his way to the top of the speaking field in a short few years.

Today, Rene travels the country sharing his story and
the concept that "no condition is permanent." Through his
humanitarian endeavors, he now feeds children, empowers
the hopeless, and acts as a light at the end of the tunnel for
countless young people in poor countries who didn't see a
way out before. The people in his impoverished village in
Haiti call him the village hero.

Every time I talk about Rene's story I'm blown away all over
again. The grinding poverty and illness of Rene's childhood
could have defeated him completely. No one would have
blamed him if right now he was curled up in a dirt hut
on the brink of death, feeling sorry for himself, shrugging
his shoulders, and thinking, "BUT there's nothing I can do
about it. That's just the way my life is."

You might say, "Sure, but look at all the breaks he got
along the way." It's true—not everyone living in poverty has
the good fortune to get the breaks that Rene got. Yet think
about that; these breaks didn't just *fall* on Rene. He noticed
them, connected with people who offered them, and forged
a chain of success one human link at a time.

If Rene had sat on his BUTS—and he had plenty of them!—he could easily have passed up the opportunity to pursue freedom, wealth, and happiness. And even if he'd made it to America, he could have stayed stuck in low-income jobs his entire life. Yet he succeeded because *every step of the way,* Rene chose to reach out and connect with all the people he came into contact with, no matter who they were, reaching for their authentic self with his own heart. When they felt that connection, they just naturally wanted to help him.

I said it in Lesson 1, and I'll say it again right now: it's the act of truly connecting—not only with other human beings, but with yourself—that is step one in getting yourself off your BUT.

LESSON 2

Watch What You Say
to Yourself!

I had just rolled into my office when the phone rang.

"Sean, you don't know me . . ." The woman on the other end of the line sounded apprehensive.

"How can I help you?"

"Well," she said timidly, "I was recently in your audience when you were delivering a speech in my town. I saw you up on stage, and saw how confident you were, and how people looked up to you and respected you, yet . . . umm . . . you looked . . ."

"Sexy?" I said playfully.

"Well," she laughed, "I was thinking more along the lines of . . . different. I mean, you're so tiny, and in that wheelchair, and yet you're larger than life. How do you do that?"

"I'm happy to share my 'magical secrets' with you," I laughed, "but tell me—why is it important for you to know this?"

"Sean, I have a daughter . . . and she's only in third grade . . ." Her voice was starting to break. ". . . and every day she comes home from school crying."

"Why?"

"She was born with a rare condition where her fingers were grown together at birth and her hands are . . . webbed, like a frog's. Her classmates call her 'weird.'" Her voice trembled, on the verge of tears. "Is there anything I can say or do to make her feel good about herself?"

My heart went out to her. "Can I talk to your daughter?"

"Oh, Sean, that would be great. Let me go get her."

My heart was pounding out of my chest. All I could think was, *I'm thousands of miles away. What the heck am I going to say to this precious child? Way to go, Motivational Man! What did you get yourself into now?*

But when I heard that girl's adorable little voice over the phone, my fears and anxiety melted away.

"Hello?" she said, sniffling.

"Hey, darling, how are you?"

"I'm all right," she whispered, with a voice that could break a giant's heart.

"Just all right, huh? Well, what's going on?"

"Um . . ." I imagined she looked at her mom for reassurance. "People call me weird and different because my hands, they look like, um . . . like frogs." Her voice trailed off in disgust.

I knew I had to do something radical to change the course of this little girl's "deformed" self-image before it got any worse.

"I'm going to ask you a very important question. Are you ready?"

"Okay."

"When people meet you, do they remember you?"

She paused for a few seconds, and then replied, "Yeah, everyone remembers me!"

"So then you're not weird, you're not different . . . you're *memorable!*"

"I am? I'm mem-or-able?" She pronounced it to rhyme with "adorable."

"That's right, sweetheart."

"Cool!" she squealed.

That's when I heard the little princess come alive in her. She began to shout, "I'm mem-or-able . . . I'm mem-or-able!"

Right away, her mother grabbed the phone. "What did you do to my daughter?" She was clearly concerned.

I explained our conversation, reassured her that her daughter was going to be just fine, and asked her to call me back in a few weeks and tell me how she was doing. I hung up the phone and drifted into deep thought . . .

The Power of Words

Words have power over us. I know—we're taught that sticks and stones may break our bones, but words will never hurt us. That's not really true. Unless you're some kind of yogi who's dedicated your life to the release of the ego, words can certainly hurt you.

Words are more than just letters squeezed together: they're packages of emotions. Loving words can make us feel wonderful. Hurtful words are toxic. Think about it: if all you did was unpack toxic packages every day, you'd eventually get sick.

Simply becoming aware of words as emotion packages can be transformational. You'll see right away that people actually do live in their language.

- Positive people use positive and uplifting words: "You look great!"
- Negative people choose negative and cynical words: "You'll never get that job. Why try?"
- People who feel victimized only use the vocabulary of victims. "I never get what I want."
- People who are always sick talk only of their sickness: "I'm just not doing very well."
- People who are extremely gracious speak only of their gratitude: "I'm so glad you were able to come today!"

It's no coincidence that good words make us feel good and that hurtful or angry words make us feel bad. There is a 100 percent correlation between the words we choose and how we feel.

GET OFF YOUR BUT *NOW!*
Pay Attention to Words

For the next twenty-four hours, I want you to pay close attention to the word choices of everyone around you. More specifically, listen to the language they use to describe

- Their feelings ("I feel like I'm trapped.")
- Their life ("I'm just hanging on by a thread.")
- How their day is going ("Same crap, different day.")
- The people in their life ("My father is an idiot.")
- Their future and their past ("I'm going nowhere fast.")

I'm betting you'll notice something right away: very happy people use a happy vocabulary, and those who are always angry use an angry vocabulary. Once you've observed people's language even for one day, it will give you a refreshing awakening to the concept that we "live in our language."

Words Can Transform

Weeks had passed since I'd spoken to the little girl with the webbed fingers. I had traveled to half a dozen states and seen thousands of people, and from time to time I wondered how she was doing. Then her mother phoned again.

"Sean . . . Sean . . . Sean! You're *never* going to believe this!" She was shouting, excited, and out of breath.

"Calm down and tell me what's going on."

"My daughter is *so* confident now!"

"That's great! What happened?" I asked.

"She marched into school and went up to all of her class-mates who were making fun of her and said, 'I'm *not* weird . . . I'm *not* different. I'm mem-or-able . . . and you're going to remember me for the *rest of your life* . . . Ha, ha, ha!' I can't thank you enough, Sean. My little angel is free to be herself."

"Wow! That's wonderful. I'm so happy to hear she's doing well. Please tell your daughter I love her and that I am so proud of her!"

After I hung up the phone, I wiped a few tears from my eyes. I was elated for many reasons, the greatest of which was the revelation about the power of words that this little girl helped me uncover. Could simply replac-ing the word "weird" with "memorable" make that big of a difference? You'd better believe it! And that was just *one* word. Think about all the other words we use to describe ourselves.

Words Can Heal, and Words Can Kill

Words hold the power to destroy, but they also hold the power to create. This is because words do more than define our experiences. In many cases they actually *create* them.

Help me finish the following phrase: "If you can't say something nice . . ."

That's right: "don't say anything at all." Most of us only think of that phrase in terms of how we talk to others. But what about how we talk to ourselves? If we say something nice to ourselves, it can be wonderful, encouraging, uplifting. And if we say something negative or critical or depressing to ourselves, it can be absolutely devastating.

What about that little voice that lives inside all of us? You know what I'm talking about. Listen. I bet you can hear it right now: "What voice? I don't have a little voice. This Sean guy is crazy. I ate too much and feel bloated. I'm tired. That girl over there doesn't like me. Did I leave the stove on?"

Yeah, that voice. It's constantly talking to us. During the day it chatters in the background, making us feel insecure or sad, and at night it narrates our dreams and nightmares and keeps us awake with worry. That voice is not something we need to be afraid of; it's something we need to take control of. Think of the voice as a two-year-old child. What would happen if a two-year-old reached out of her highchair for more dessert and you ignored her? Maybe she would scream and cry until you at least paid attention to her. Sadly, this is what happens to our internal voice. I have found that most people never deal with their inner voice until it gets too loud and starts acting disrespectful.

To escape this internal turmoil, we often numb ourselves into oblivion by overeating, watching too much TV, having impersonal sex, drinking too much alcohol, using drugs . . . the list goes on. For some people, the inner voice gets so hurtful that they believe that the only way they can shut it off is by taking their own life. This is not the outcome I want for you or anyone else in the world.

Parenting Our Inner Voice

Like good parents of demanding two-year-olds, we need to take control and start parenting our inner voice. Would you talk to your child or best friend the way you sometimes talk to yourself? I didn't think so.

If we catch ourselves saying mean things to ourselves—"You're too fat! No one will ever love you! You can't do anything right!"—we have to intervene and say, "I'm sorry. I didn't mean that. I'm just a little [tired, scared, overwhelmed] right now." Apologizing to ourselves is a foreign concept, but it's necessary.

We must respect ourselves. Practice talking to yourself the way you would talk to a best friend, a mentor, or someone you really look up to. Trust me, life will place plenty of obstacles in your path. You can't afford to be one of them yourself.

Be Your Own Best Friend

I've been fascinated with self-talk ever since I became a therapist. It's a dialogue that we rarely listen to consciously. Why? Maybe because we're too distracted by ourselves, being critical and negative about who we are and what we're doing. Meanwhile, our own inner voice is doing a hatchet job on us.

It's true: if you talked to your friends the way you talk to yourself, you probably wouldn't have any friends. I have worked with enough people to know for sure that we are harder on ourselves—and meaner—than we are to anyone else.

It's silly to worry about what others might be saying and thinking about you. Whatever they're saying, it's not really about you—it's about them. In fact, what people say or think about you is a direct reflection of what they may be feeling about themselves. Don't even think about it. If you want something to concentrate on, concentrate on treating yourself with more respect.

How Words Impact Our Self-Confidence

When I sit down with a male client who's struggling in his dating life, I ask him about what he's saying to himself.

Here are some examples I hear over and over:

"I'd do better with girls, BUT I'm too ugly."

"I'd ask out more girls, BUT I'm not confident enough."

"I would have asked for her phone number, BUT she could do better than me."

We really do sabotage ourselves with the dark sound-track we have looping over and over in our minds. Whenever I hear this negative self-talk from clients, I say, "You *must* turn off the horrific noise going on in your head."

"BUT Sean," they often say, "it's too hard to stop that voice from saying mean things."

My reply is always the same: "It will be much harder if you don't."

Sadly, I am no longer surprised to find that men around the world beat themselves up internally, especially in the area of dating. My online magazine for men, *InnerGameMagazine.com*, is an educational forum designed to help guys learn how to develop into confident, proud, successful, and genuine men. Every day, we get e-mail from men struggling with what I call "inner game dysfunction."

One young guy started right off by identifying himself as "a loser, a big-time loser." He said he was good looking and not perceived as a loser by society, but that he always held back in relationships because he felt that he wasn't "good enough." What this man didn't know was that he was far from alone in his feelings, and far from alone in his negative self-talk!

I explained that he needed to turn around his self-talk. What was hurting him more than anything he listed in his letter—at twenty-two, he was living with his parents, in debt, and out of work—was the limiting label that he'd been identifying with most of his life: "I'm a loser." I can't think of a more unattractive phrase! If you tell yourself every day that you're a loser, those you're attracted to will sense this on a deep intuitive level and want nothing to do with you. It's as simple (and brutal) as that.

The Hammer Versus the Doormat

A few years back, I was speaking at a leadership development conference for college students, which was attended by thousands of members of national fraternities and sororities. After my presentation, the room emptied out and I was left with only a few stragglers. We took seats on the stage and delved deep into conversation about the topics I had discussed in my program.

After a few minutes, a young woman in the group opened up.

"I'm tired of being a doormat," she began.

"What does 'doormat' mean to you?"

She got quiet. Her nose turned bright red, her upper lip began to quiver, and pain welled up in her eyes and streamed down her face as tears. She could hardly catch her breath, but she said, "A doormat is something everyone walks all over." She gasped for a breath and continued.

"A doormat is something everyone uses and then leaves behind." By this point she was sobbing. "Everyone leaves their dirt on me."

We were no longer talking in metaphorical terms, we were deep into her personal situation. She was clearly telling herself terrible things. Her self-talk was so critical and negative. Worse, she was oblivious to the fact that she was locked in a linguistic torture chamber.

Then I asked her, "What's the opposite of a doormat?"

She thought a minute and said, "A hammer."

"Okay, why a hammer?"

"No one can abuse a hammer. It's tough. It's inde-structible, you know?"

"I hear you. What else is important about a hammer?"

"Well, a hammer is strong and constructive . . . Oh." She stopped and looked up at the ceiling and smiled.

It later came out in the conversation that she had been calling herself a doormat for years. She had actually incorporated this one word into her identity, automatically assuming the doormat role in her interactions with the people in her life. Now, however, she had a new word: hammer. I could see her life begin to change right before my eyes.

Choose the words you say to yourself wisely: they are creating your reality.

GET OFF YOUR BUT *NOW!*
Eavesdrop on Yourself

Even though we all know it's wrong, it's hard not to lis-ten in on someone else's conversation. You know what I am talking about. You're at a restaurant, and you over-hear a couple at the table behind you breaking up. You strain to listen to what they're saying. As impolite as eavesdropping may be, we've all been guilty of it from time to time. Put this skill to work! Start eavesdropping on the conversation you're having with yourself.

1. Spend one day simply noticing what you say to your-self. Write it down in your Get Off Your BUT Now! journal as you go through the day. Do not alter or judge these statements. Simply observe them and write them down as if you were a clinical scientist.

2. The next day, review these statements. Ask yourself, Would I say this to my best friend, my boss, my child, or my mentor? Would I be embarrassed if others knew I was saying these things to myself? Is what I am saying to myself encouraging me to grow or weighing me down?

3. Write down a list of ten things you would like to start saying to yourself.

Start repeating these statements as often as you like. Notice that as you do, your overall feeling about life and yourself can't help but change.

Remember: we can't change what we don't acknowl-edge. That's why it's important to pay attention to that little voice that's always talking inside our heads. The eavesdrop-ping activity always amazes people. Even those who think of themselves as positive and upbeat often find that their inner monologue presents the extreme opposite. Once you start listening to that persistent voice, you'll be surprised by how often you'll catch yourself saying mean things to and about yourself. Keep listening! Eventually, with practice, you'll start replacing the negative phrases with empowering ones automatically.

GET OFF YOUR BUT NOW!
Replace Your Negative Self-Chatter with an Uplifting Voice

Replacing your negative chatter with an uplifting voice is going to take some practice. Here's a successful activity I do whenever I'm stuck in a negative self-talk loop.

1. Take three deep breaths in through your nose and let them out through your mouth as slowly as possible. Think only about your breathing. Visualize the air coming into your lungs as a soothing color, and returning out through your mouth as an even brighter and more soothing color. Even if this all sounds a bit New Age "woo-woo," do it anyway.

2. Pick one word or phrase that lifts you up, something that empowers you, a phrase that makes you feel that you are unstoppable and the most loved person on this planet. For me that phrase is "I am infinite!"

3. Visualize an image that correlates with your empowering phrase and really see it: make it even bigger
and brighter in the movie screen in your mind.

4. You should already be in a better state of mind than
you were before you started this exercise, so this is a
good time to have a heart-to-heart discussion with
yourself. Tell yourself all the empowering things you
need to hear, words you wish your family, friends,
coworkers, and lovers would say to you. (You might
find some on your list of ten positive self-talk phrases
from the last activity.) This is not about "positive
affirmations": this is all about becoming your own
greatest support system.

The BUT Triple Threat

Most negative self-talk centers around three specific language patterns I call the BUT triple threat:

- BUT fears
- BUT excuses
- BUT insecurities

These three patterns have the power to mire any person in a feeling of absolute and total hopelessness. Let's take
a closer look at how you can deal with each of them.

Dealing with Your BUT Fears

Have you ever noticed that whenever you find yourself in a new situation and you're not certain of the outcome, it feels natural to be afraid? Your heart starts to race, your stomach does acrobatics, and you begin sweating in places you didn't even know you had. That's also when your negative self-talk often kicks in:

"BUT what if I fail?"

"BUT what if I look bad?"

"BUT what if I disappoint everyone?"

Just about any phrase that starts off with "BUT what if . . ." is simply fear attempting to work its way into your life. You can't rent it one square inch in your mind, or it will squat on the property and turn that magnificent mansion into a dark, warped, and dangerous crack house. Fear running free in your self-talk must be stopped in its tracks immediately upon recognition.

This acronym has been used so much it's a cliché—but clichés are clichés because they tend to be true. So here it is again. FEAR is

False

Experiences

Appearing

Real

That's all it is. Think about it: How many of the things you've been afraid of in your life have come to pass? Not many, if any, right? It's purely a waste of your time and energy and emotion to worry, "BUT what if . . ."!

Instead, step in and ask yourself these questions:

"What if my fear is wrong?"

"Who *says* this fear is true?"

"What if the best-case scenario plays out instead of my worst-case fear?"

Fear cripples us. I once met a young woman who was so crippled by fear that she was afraid to drive, go swimming, and use public restrooms and elevators. By running an endless loop of worst-case scenarios in her mind, she literally talked herself into panic attacks on a daily basis.

This young woman had grown up in a household where her mom was *always* worried that something bad could happen. Many times over the years, her mom would cancel all their family plans out of pure, unfounded fear. As we worked together, I learned that she loved her mom dearly. Deep down inside, she was afraid that if she didn't share or live out her mom's paranoia, she would be acting as if her mom were flawed. If instead she exhibited the same patterns of fear, she could feel that her mom was no different from her. So she lived in a tiny reality where she could hardly go anywhere without being afraid.

Once we started tweaking her "BUT what if . . ." fears, her reality shifted. I explained that every time she had a fearful thought, she should stop and ask herself these four questions:

1. What would happen if that did happen?
2. What wouldn't happen if that did happen?
3. What would happen if this didn't happen?
4. What wouldn't happen if this didn't happen?

It's magic! This repetitious neuro-linguistic pattern actually scrambles the fear. When you order your mind to stop obsessing on the worst-case scenario and put it to work finding alternative outcomes, it gets distracted. And by the time your brain processes the fourth question, it has no choice but to lose its grip on the fear.

I use this formula every time I find myself frozen in a romantic dating scenario. If I'm at a dance club or bookstore and I see a young woman I want to approach, yet my brain produces a "BUT what if . . ." fear, I immediately step in and scramble the pattern so that I can get unstuck. Only then am I able to relax and be myself. We're so afraid of looking bad that we forget no one's looking at us—just like you, other people are looking at who's looking at them.

Bottom line? "BUT what if . . ." fears are a complete waste of your time. Nine times out of ten, whatever you're afraid of is not dangerous or life threatening. In fact, it's probably not even real.

Dealing with BUT Excuses

BUT excuses can swim into self-talk on an hourly basis if
we aren't careful. A BUT excuse is based on an imaginary
lack of resources that leads to the belief that we can't do
what needs to be done.

The BUT excuse is always stated as a fact, and we may
actually *believe* it's a fact. But it's really just an excuse we use
to rationalize our lack of activity or participation:

"BUT I don't have the time!"

"BUT I don't have the money!"

"BUT I don't have the energy!"

Why do we like these BUT excuses so much? Because
a BUT excuse gets us out of doing things we don't want
to do. In the beginning, sitting on our BUT excuses can
be really comfortable. People leave us alone. Eventually,
though, that's all they ever leave us.

Here's an example. Your friend asks you a dozen times,
"You want to come to the gym with me this week?"

"I would love to," you reply sweetly, "BUT I don't
have the money for a fitness membership."

Another victory recorded in your "I can get out of
anything" game, right?

Wrong!

BUT excuses always come back to haunt us. We skip
the gym, leaving more time for mindless TV channel surfing,
and our body suffers. We get stiffer and more out of shape, and

start packing on the pounds. Meanwhile, we cry that if we just had better genes, we would *already* be physically fit and trim.

I know this doesn't sound very pretty. But we all need to hear it. I'm as guilty of embracing my BUT excuses as anyone else. The goal is not to be perfect—our minds are experts at coming up with excuses. The real goal is to recognize when you're stuck in a BUT excuse loop and do something to get out of it!

Here's a secret: the excuse itself is never the real reason behind our inaction; it's just a cover-up for something we're unwilling to face up to. The truth is that for some other reason that we may not want to acknowledge, we really don't want that "something"—going to the gym, returning to school, finding a new job, or whatever it is—to be part of our current reality. Our BUT excuse masks our true feelings, which may be something like

"I hate working out because I feel fat at the gym."

"I don't want to go back to school because it's just too hard and I don't think I can hack it."

"I'm not interested in dating because I don't want to risk being dumped."

These true feelings are never easy to acknowledge, and often we may even be ashamed of them. We hide behind our BUT excuses so that everyone else will leave us alone. And that's how an individual can end up alone in life.

"Okay, Sean, I get it! How do I get off my BUT excuses?"

Here's what I do:

1. I get 100 percent honest with myself. I reveal things that I don't want to hear, see, or feel, even if it makes me uncomfortable in the moment.
2. I project my current behavior out into future. What will happen if I don't change now? Next week? Next month? Next year? In ten years? The answer is never warm and fuzzy, but it's always motivating!

Get honest with yourself and change your behavior.

Dealing with Your BUT Insecurities

Our BUT insecurities go right for our self-esteem. These insecurities lurk deep inside, ready and waiting to do you in. In fact, when you think you're doing really great, they can pop up to pull you down:

"BUT I'm not attractive enough."

"BUT I'm not smart enough."

"BUT I'm not talented enough."

When we sell ourselves the lie that we're not "enough" or that we're flawed or broken in some way, we short-circuit all our hopes and dreams. This kind of self-talk defeats us before we even begin, and makes it virtually impossible for us to look in the mirror and see the whole human being who's really there.

It also makes it impossible for our friends to help us. I once broke up with a girl because her BUT insecurities were drowning her. It was like walking through quicksand. No matter what I did to try to help her get out of her destructive self-talk loop, she slipped deeper into her own personal hell.

Good lesson for me! That's the interesting thing about our BUTS: no one can get us off of them except ourselves. You can throw people a rope, but if they refuse to grab on and pull their own weight, you can't save them. Ultimately, it's their choice. Sadly, the longer I stuck around this girl, the more she pulled me down with her.

Where do insecurities come from, how do they form, and how can we get rid of them? In order to answer these questions, we first need to understand how beliefs work.

How Beliefs Work

The only difference between a thought (which really doesn't have much power over you) and a belief (which has total control over you) is this: a belief is a thought you've convinced yourself is true. In other words . . .

A belief is just a thought that you've made real.

Studies indicate that we have more than forty thousand thoughts per day. (I feel bad for the person who had to count each one of them!) Most of our thoughts are fairly insignificant. A handful of thoughts, however, can be powerful. These are the thoughts we deem as "truth,"

the ones that become our beliefs. A belief has only one job:
to gather evidence for its existence. Once our mind decides,
"Yep, that's true," it (our mind) will go out into the world
and find evidence to back it (our belief) up—even if it
(our mind) has to delete, distort, generalize, or even fabri-
cate every bit of evidence it (our mind) gathers to prove its
(our beliefs) own existence.

The Greatest Lie Ever Told

I'm sure you've heard the phrase "Seeing is believing." Well,
I have some bad news. You've been lied to. Seeing is NOT
believing. It's the other way around: believing is seeing.
Whatever you really believe about something, your brain
will alter your five senses so that you actually experience it
as real and true.

Here's a vivid example I have seen in both my speaking and therapy careers. I have worked with gorgeous
young women who could easily be models, yet they feel
ugly. How is that even possible? Aren't they looking in the
mirror? But if you remember the phrase "Believing is seeing," it all becomes clear. If we believe we are unattractive,
our brain will work full-time—in every waking second—
to make sure all the sincere compliments we receive about
our appearance are distorted or deleted as they enter our
consciousness. Thus we never even hear the compliment, or
we reject it immediately as flattery designed to get us to do
something.

How Beliefs Take Root in Our Mind

Here's a visual for how a belief works.

Imagine an acorn. Can you see it?

A thought is like that acorn. By itself, it is a solid little object that can't do much. If you keep it in a tin can, it will never grow. But if you plant it in soil and give it the right amount of sun, nutrients, and water, it will sprout roots and grow into a huge oak tree. In order for a thought to become a belief, it has to be nurtured by evidence that proves its own existence. With each piece of evidence, it sprouts a root, and its foundation grows stronger. Soon, that thought—true or false—becomes a sturdy belief planted in your mind, growing stronger every day.

Beliefs aren't inherently bad or good. They are just "gofers" for whatever we want to bring into our reality. If we ask our belief that we are beautiful, for example, to go gather evidence to support it, it will find every shred of proof it can to convince us that we are beautiful. That's empowering! Unfortunately, it will do the same for the limiting belief that we are unattractive.

The quality of your beliefs and the self-talk that supports those beliefs determine the quality of your emotions. If you spend your time proving that you're ugly, dumb, not supposed to be wealthy, and defective, I promise you that your emotional state is going to be depressed and angry, and all your negative self-talk will create a terrible state of mind. To counter the emotional pain this causes, many of us turn to immediate gratification—food, alcohol, drugs, and so on. But none of those gratifiers give us lasting satisfaction. Lasting gratification comes only from growth and contribution. It's only when we work on ourselves and we contribute our resources (time, money, and energy) to the efforts of others or the planet are we truly blessed with lasting gratification.

GET OFF YOUR BUT *NOW!*
Make a "Get Off Your BUT" Personal Inventory

Beliefs are so powerful that they determine everything from our daily habits to our long-term goals. Why not discover right now what you really believe about yourself, your body, your job, your relationship, your future? Take out your Get Off Your BUT Now! journal and finish the following statements—in as much detail as possible—with whatever comes up for you, no matter how pretty or ugly it may sound.

- Men are _____.
- Women are _____.
- My body is _____.
- My career is _____.
- My future looks _____.
- My partner is _____.
- I'm good at _____.
- I'm lousy at _____.

- People think I am _____.
- When I am under pressure, I _____.
- The world is _____.
- What I love about people is _____.
- What I hate about people is _____.
- My heart is _____.
- Marriage is _____.
- Love is _____.
- Exercise is _____.
- Work is _____.
- Life is _____.

Interesting stuff, huh? Writing down what's in our hearts and heads can sometimes be startling to read. The first time I did this assignment, I was shocked to discover what I believed. Fortunately, you can change your beliefs!

You can't change what you won't or haven't acknowledged—and that's why this exercise is so helpful. Sometimes, simply acknowledging a belief is enough for you to be able to let it go. If you don't like a particular belief you discovered in this inventory, write about what you *do* want to believe. Once you've described your new belief in detail, you'll have it in your mind. Then you can begin to find evidence in your life to support that new belief.

Are you beginning to see the value in every word you choose to tell yourself? I hope so! Your self-talk creates the map that directs your life. The question is, what route are you mapping out?

We often think that we have to "find" ourselves in life. Yet we don't have to search the world to find ourselves. We *create* ourselves every moment, and we do so through our language, through what we say to ourselves on a regular basis.

You can't afford to treat yourself as anything less than the coolest person on the planet. Does it seem foreign to speak lovingly to yourself? Try it anyway. I promise, your life will become *amazing* when you do. How do I know? Because I vowed years ago to always speak to myself with love and respect, and I am one of the happiest and most peaceful people you'll ever meet. You see, when you combine respectful self-talk with physical confidence (we'll talk about that in the next lesson), people will begin loving and respecting you on a level you never thought possible.

That's right! It's not only how you think about yourself inside that counts. Your confidence also manifests on the outside, in how you carry yourself. In fact, simply by presenting yourself as confident—no matter how you may feel on the inside—you will not only convince others; ultimately, you will convince the most important person: yourself.

HOW BOBBY GOT OFF HIS BUT

"I would move on with my life, BUT a drunk driver killed my wife."

The words you use to make sense of your experiences are profound: they truly do determine whether you get off your BUT. Perhaps no one understands this better than my friend Bobby. He's the kind of guy who doesn't have a cross word to say about anything or anyone. Every time we hang out, he's wearing a big smile, sharing upbeat stories, and reflecting with gratitude. When I'm around him, I can't help but feel grateful too. Maybe that doesn't sound very impressive—a nice guy who makes people feel good—but I bet it will after you read about what he went through in his life some years ago, long before I became his friend.

In 1985, Bobby Petrocelli thought he had it all: a great job coaching sports in a sports-crazy Texas high school, and his two-and-half-year marriage to his beautiful wife, Ava, the love of his life. That night, he got home about 10:30 PM and ate a big bowl of rigatoni, another of his loves. He and Ava nestled close on the sofa as they always did, and talked softly about how their day had gone and the approaching Thanksgiving and Christmas holidays. When they went to sleep that night, they couldn't have been happier.

The next thing Bobby knew, he was looking at the headlights of a pickup truck. A man stepped out of the truck and asked, "Is there anyone else in the house?" Bobby looked around. His bed was gone. Ava was gone. The smell of tar and burning rubber filled his bedroom.

The driver of the three-quarter-ton pickup truck had been drinking that night. In fact, he was drunk—he had a blood alcohol content of 0.19, almost twice the legal limit. He'd sped at 70 mph across a grassy field, traveling 313 feet—more than the length of a football field—and smashed straight through the brick wall of Bobby's house. As the truck hit the concrete foundation slab, it went airborne for an instant, landing on Bobby and Ava as they were sleeping. The truck landed right on top of Bobby, running him over completely. The tires, still spinning, burned hot rubber into his leg, back, and abdomen. Then the truck kept going, throwing him on top of the hood and carrying him out of the bedroom and twenty-five feet through the house into the dining room, where his face shattered the window.

While Bobby was riding on the hood of the truck, Ava was underneath it, rolled up in the sheets and a mattress. As the truck plowed through the house, it dragged Ava along. Later, Bobby learned that when the truck landed on her, it most likely knocked the air out of her body. Simultaneously, the sheets and the mattress wrapped around her face and body so tightly that she never got another breath of air. She died of suffocation, wrapped in the sheets of their bed. It took thirty minutes to dig her body out from underneath the rubble. When they found her, she didn't have a single scratch on her or even one broken bone.

From start to finish, the accident had taken about ten seconds. All of Bobby's hopes and dreams for a happy marriage and future with Ava were gone. All he could think about was that ten seconds. Ten seconds can change a life forever.

The next several months were very, very difficult. Every time he took off his shirt, he saw the scars left by tire tracks across his body. He did what anyone would do to save his sanity: he went into denial and shock. Bobby was numb, refusing to accept the fact that the tragedy had taken place. Eventually, however, the shock wore off, and he felt his pain head-on. For a while, he wrapped his pain around him like a blanket, justifying it by saying to himself, "I would let go of this pain, BUT that would be dishonoring Ava." Sadly, the longer he sat back on this BUT, the weaker he felt. Finally, even through his sadness and despair, he understood that holding on to his sadness and anger was not healing in any way. Maybe holding on to her memory really meant letting go.

He stopped talking to himself about dishonoring Ava and started thinking about honoring her instead. To Bobby, that meant speaking about how he felt rather than giving himself BUT excuses not to talk at all. He began to open up and talk to family and friends about his true feelings, his confusion and his pain. He was no longer afraid to cry if he felt he needed to. This release eventually allowed him to begin to move on—in a way he never expected.

Bobby found that speaking positively was so empowering that he began to want to share his story with others outside his personal circle. So Bobby volunteered with

youth organizations, such as Students Against Drunk
Driving and the Fellowship of Christian Athletes, which he
had sponsored in Santa Fe. The more he shared, the more
he felt in his heart that his life had been spared for just
this purpose: so that he could share with young people the
dangers of drinking and driving. Now his healing began in
earnest. Instead of focusing on the scars from the accident
that covered his body, he started to exercise again, getting
back into shape and feeling more confident.

　　There was one more thing, however. Bobby had to forgive the man who caused this tragedy. Forgiving him didn't
mean that he was letting him off the hook or that it was okay
that he'd killed Ava, either. It didn't mean that he shouldn't
have to pay back something to society. But Bobby knew he
had to forgive this man so that he himself could be free—
from the hatred and bitterness that could enslave him for the
rest of his life. When Bobby finally said the words, "I forgive
you," to the man who drove a truck through his perfect life,
he felt a burden being lifted from his shoulders. It was the
last of his anger, floating away. He began to heal for good.

　　By 1986, Bobby realized that making a fresh start would
mean leaving Texas and moving back home, to New York.
He didn't know what lay ahead, but he felt peaceful about
taking that step. Soon he found a job teaching and coaching. The school asked Bobby to share his story at a large
assembly. Since then, Bobby has gone on to speak in hundreds of assemblies every year. Over one million people
have now seen him share his story live.

Once, I asked Bobby, "Were you afraid you'd never find love again?"

"Actually, Sean, I was haunted more by the thought that I'd never be able to love again. However, one day I met a beautiful young woman." Like Bobby, she was an athlete. Three years later, on May 6, 1989, they were married and soon had two beautiful boys.

Today Bobby is one of the most sought-after motivational speakers in the country. He has authored several books, including his autobiography, *10 Seconds*. Beyond his message about the dangers of drinking and driving, he feels that the most important message he can share is that, "Each decision has the power to affect not only us but also the lives of others." Choose wisely.

I know my friend Bobby's situation was horrific—worse than anything most people ever have to experience. However, I decided to share it with you because I wanted you to see the tremendous power—both positive and negative—of the words we say to ourselves. Even in the worst of circumstances, as this truly was, you can still push forward.

When the world feels as if it's falling apart around you, you need to be your own best friend. Give yourself the best advice you have! Choose the words you use wisely: they will play and replay in your mind for years on end.

And Bobby didn't think only about the words he said to himself but also about the messages he gave himself at every opportunity. "Sean," Bobby once told me, "the only reason I was able to survive and rebuild after that accident was because I immersed myself in uplifting thoughts, words, and beliefs." He read inspiring passages from scripture, watched funny movies, and devoured personal development literature. It all contributed to freeing Bobby from his darkness.

In my years of traveling the world, I've heard hundreds of tear-filled stories. I've hugged complete strangers as they've sobbed in my arms. I always whisper the same thing to them: "Look for the gift in your pain."

If you look for that gift, believe me, you will find it. If you don't look, it's all too easy to become enslaved by your misery. Bobby could so easily have fallen victim to being a victim. Who wouldn't have agreed with him if he had shrugged and said, "I would date again, BUT my one and only soul mate was unfairly torn out of my life." Or, "I would move on with my life, BUT my body is permanently scarred with the daily reminder of the worst day of my life."

Our toughest BUTS leave us feeling isolated from the world, feeling as if no one could possibly understand us, let alone help us. The BUTS we sit on after tragedies are some of the most dangerous ones because those who love us feel impotent to help us. They can't possibly understand what we're going through, so they leave us to wallow in our pain.

Well, I refuse to be one of those people who are afraid to rock your boat! I'm here to shake your soul out of its misery. Your life has much more to offer you than you've yet experienced. Now is the time to brush off the negative thoughts and beliefs you've been carrying for too long.

LESSON 3

Master Your Physical Confidence

How you move, speak, look, and carry yourself plays a crucial part not only in determining how others perceive you but also in building your own sense of confidence and self-worth. I witnessed a great example of this at an early age, when I got to meet the most confident man I'd ever seen.

When this man walked into the room, my eyes widened. His presence was larger than life. It didn't hurt that he was six foot seven and as broad as a refrigerator. (The only thing missing was his giant blue ox.) He spoke to me, but I could hardly concentrate on what he was saying. It didn't seem real. I was starstruck, slightly intimidated, and overjoyed—all at the same time. Hey, it's not often in life you get to stand eye to eye (or eye to kneecap, in this case) with your childhood hero . . . But I'm getting ahead of myself. Allow me to rewind the film of my life and share with you how my first meeting with Tony Robbins came about.

Sean's Childhood Wish Comes True

While I was in college, my friends were busy spending any
money they had on pizza, beer, and car payments. Not me.
I saved up my money and bought the latest personal growth
tape series from Anthony Robbins. My fascination with this
king of self-development had begun when I was a kid.
With all the air travel my family and I did, I developed a
bond with the grown-up gift catalog that always seemed to
be tucked away in the seatback pocket in front of me. What
especially turned me on were the ads for audio albums by
a man named Anthony Robbins. Phrases like "live with passion," "awaken the giant within," and "personal power"
leaped out at me.

The sales copy alone motivated me. Robbins made
bold claims: "You can have anything you want in life!" and
"You control the course of your destiny!" His optimism
was intoxicating. As I got older, I would sometimes catch
his late-night infomercials on TV. I just knew that somehow,
some way, I was going to meet and befriend this self-help
giant. Then, in late June 1996, when I became governor
of Illinois Boys State, I got my chance to set the wheels in
motion.

That year, I was offered a teenage boy's dream come
true—the opportunity to address the entire population
of that year's Illinois Girls State. I've delivered hundreds of
talks to thousands of people throughout the course of my

career as a speaker. Few, however—if any—have topped that one. I brought the house down. These teenage girls (close to a thousand) had been cooped up all week with no boys in sight. I was the first contact they had had with a guy in what probably felt like ages to them. For fifteen minutes and thirty-seven seconds, I got to be Elvis.

After my speech, a girl named Jeanine approached me. We totally hit it off. A week later, she invited me to attend the Miss Illinois pageant with her. She wanted to support her friend, who was a contestant. During the pageant we got a little bored, so we sneaked out the back door and joked around in the lobby. While we were busy horsing around, a man in his mid-forties approached us.

"My name is John," he said. He was very curious to know what my disability was and what challenges I had faced because of it. I figured he was just a friendly guy who was curious about my physical condition. I'd met scores of people like that. At the moment, however, I was slightly annoyed at this interruption—I was busy flirting with Jeanine.

Then he let me know that he was a frequent volunteer for the Make-A-Wish Foundation. He told me I was probably entitled to a wish because of my life-altering disability. I said, sure. Hey, why not? Finally he left, and Jeanine and I went back to having fun.

John never forgot his promise. Although it took more than two years to arrange (mostly because of Tony's schedule and my own increasingly packed one), I got my wish. I was flown to Orlando, Florida, to meet Tony Robbins one-on-one after one of his live events.

Gifts from Tony Robbins

As he walked in the door, his presence filled the room. I had met only one other person on the planet who could captivate an audience with just his sheer persona—President Clinton.

"Nice to finally meet you, Sean," Tony said. His voice was deep enough to make a radio disc jockey feel inadequate.

"The pleasure is all mine, Mr. Robbins."

"Call me Tony."

"Okay, Mr. Tony," I said, joking around.

Tony could see that my face was covered with acne; I was slouched in my wheelchair in an uncomfortable position (due to my back pain); and I knew I looked exhausted. You could hear in his voice his concern for my health. He said, "Sean, I don't believe you have to be in this much pain. If you're interested, I'd like to put you in contact with an individual who dramatically improved my health and wellness through dietary changes."

Sure, why not?

But I had so much more I wanted to ask him, and I didn't know whether I'd ever get another chance—or even how much of one I had with him now. I figured it was probably about fifteen more minutes, tops. So I thought quickly on my wheels. I asked him to take his watch off, place it face down on the coffee table, and continue chatting with me for a little while longer. He smiled and then willingly obliged. To this day, he proudly shares how brave he thought this request was from a kid to a man four times his size and more than twenty years his senior.

A few weeks later, I flew to Utah to meet with Tony's health adviser, Dr. Robert Young. Dr. Young helped permanently alleviate my back pain, cleared up my acne, and strengthened my bones.

Although my health changes didn't "cure" me of my physical condition, I can say with joy that I haven't fractured any bones since I met Tony more than ten years ago. This is quite amazing, considering that I'm not on bone density medications—or any medications, for that matter.

My new state of good health was transformational in other areas of my life as well, and allowed me to take full advantage of one more introduction Tony gave me. This introduction was not to a person but to a new way of being that empowered me to move forward on this planet boldly and with great purpose: the concept of physical confidence. I would be honored to introduce you to your own physical confidence—right now.

GET OFF YOUR BUT *NOW!*
Modeling Physical Confidence

As I worked alongside both Tony Robbins and Bill Clinton, I couldn't help noticing that everything they did conveyed the same message: "I carry power." They absolutely radiated physical confidence. I wanted what they had. So I tried to model myself on them.

Now I want *you* to find a confident role model—someone you know, or a person you can observe through film or TV. Pay close attention to the following:

1. The way this person moves.
2. The way he or she stands.
3. The way he or she sits.
4. The way he or she speaks.

Observe every detail about this role model's body language—how he or she moves and holds himself or herself during these activities. If you want to take notes, do that. Now close your eyes and see yourself moving in the same way. You'll feel a new sense of power in your body right away, and you may also find your posture changing to adjust to the picture in your mind.

Keep practicing. Remember: it's not about mimicking, like a parrot, without really understanding. It's about allowing yourself to follow a model—the way you would try to swing a golf club the way Tiger Woods does in order to teach your body a more effective golf swing. Your goal is to integrate these confident ways of moving into the way your own body moves.

The Mind-Body Connection

Physical confidence is the external expression of our internal state of confidence. In simpler terms, it is how confidence looks and sounds.

Think of the most confident person you know. Think back to the first time you met him or her. How quickly did you know that this person was confident? I'm guessing that it took less than a few seconds. Probably more like milliseconds. Now think of the most insecure and fearful person you've ever met. How quickly could you tell that he or she was NOT confident? I'm guessing that it was the same amount of time. All you had to do was take one look and you knew.

How is it possible that we can spot a confident person from across the room? Because to a great degree, we wear our confidence on the outside.

Think about it: When you're feeling depressed, what direction does your head naturally point? That's right, down. When you're scared, do you naturally take deep or shallow breaths? Yep, shallow. Does smiling make you happy, or does happiness make you smile? Hmm . . .

The mind and body may seem like two separate entities. In reality, however, they are one. Whenever something happens to you psychologically, you experience an instantaneous physiological reaction. Conversely, when you introduce any stimulation to the body, you instantaneously experience an intellectual and emotional reaction.

Have you ever been so worried about something that you got sick to your stomach? That's possible because your entire body (not just the brain) is a thinking and feeling machine. Research shows that even the most microscopic parts of you (cells, molecules, atoms, quarks) are working together in constant communication.

Our nervous and digestive systems in particular are so closely linked that many researchers refer to them as one physical unit: the brain-gut axis. Your gut actually contains as many neurons (nerve cells) as your spinal cord does. This connection between the brain and the digestive system is an extremely busy two-way street. The central nervous system releases chemicals (acetylcholine and adrenaline) that tell the stomach when to produce acid, when to churn, and when to rest. Our digestive system responds by sending electrical messages to the brain, creating such sensations as hunger, fullness, pain, nausea, discomfort—and, possibly, such emotions as sadness and joy.

The Brain-Gut Axis

According to Emeran Mayer, MD, a gastroenterologist and the chairman of the new Mind-Body Collaborative Research Center at the University of California at Los Angeles, our guts actually help shape our moods. Especially important, according to Dr. Mayer, is the vagus nerve, which is essentially a large electrical cable that runs between the brain and the digestive system.

"Doctors once believed the nerve's main job was controlling acid production in the stomach," he says. "But 95 percent of the fibers go the other direction—from the gut to the brain."[1]

Nobody knows exactly what messages are traveling along this cable, but scientists have found that stimulating the nerve at different frequencies can cause either anxiety or a strong sense of well-being. Perhaps the term "gut feeling" isn't just a figure of speech after all.

So what does the brain-gut axis have to do with physical confidence? The existence of this pathway is proof that our body really does have a direct impact on our mind. So we must take care that our body's posture and movements signal to the brain that we are in control, at peace, and excited about our future.

The body is a powerful yet delicate instrument. We can do a lot with it, especially when we feel good. When those feel-good chemicals are pumping to your brain, you feel good. When you give your body the right fuel, you feel good.

And when you keep your muscles tuned up, you feel good! So if you want to exude physical confidence, it's best to stay in shape. It's important to take good care of your body—you only get one. As busy as I am, I'm always making time to work out, stretch, stay hydrated, and eat well. If you do the same, your physical confidence will shine even more brightly around others.

GET OFF YOUR BUT *NOW!*
Shift Your Body, Shift Your Mind

Have you ever been in a bad mood and wanted to get out of it because you had pressing obligations, but you felt stuck in the negative emotion—mired in the anger, sadness, fear, hurt, or guilt? Positive affirmations are generally useless in these circumstances, "I'm happy . . . I'm happy . . . I'm happy . . . " Yeah, sure you are.

But Tony Robbins has taught me that *you can shift your state of mind by shifting your body.* Or, as he puts it, "Motion creates Emotion!" If you spark the body, you spark the mind. The E in emotion in this case stands for energy. In other words, an emotion is "energy in motion." Place this book in front of you so that you can read these directions and follow along at the same time:

1. Put your body in a posture that conveys fear. Move your head, face, shoulders, arms, hands, chest, and

legs into the position that feels most like fear. Even breathe like someone who is afraid.

2. Freeze your body in that exact fearful position. Don't move a single muscle.

3. Now try getting super excited, feeling really pumped up and confident, as if you could take on the world.

4. Notice the conflict you're experiencing between these contradictory emotions.

5. Shake your body out and brush off the fearful energy you created with your posture. Take a deep breath and then let out a sigh of relief.

6. Now pose your body in a posture that conveys confidence and power. Move your head, face, shoulders, arms, hands, chest, and legs into the position that makes you feel most confident and powerful. Even breathe like someone who is confident and powerful.

7. Freeze your body in that exact confident and powerful position. Don't move a single muscle.

8. Now try feeling really timid and fearful, as if you were afraid of your own shadow.

9. Notice how it's not possible to do step 8 without shifting your body.

This activity is a powerful demonstration that every emotion has a correlating physiological position. If you want to shift your emotions, you must shift your physiology.

Physical Confidence Is Vital

Next time you're in a bad mood, stop and check in with
your body. If you're feeling angry, notice how your body
is in an angry posture (fists clenched, shoulders hunched,
lips in a tight line), your voice has an angry tone, and you
breathe at a fast, ragged, angry rate. If you wanted to,
you could intervene at any time and feel something different—simply by shifting your body into a happy posture:
hands open, shoulders down, mouth curving upward in a
smile, voice with a more upbeat tonality, breathing relaxed.
Like magic, you'd feel better.

Of course, I'm not saying that this shift of physiology
will fix the problem of whatever angered you in the first place.
What it will do is decrease or possibly eliminate the intensity
of the sensation of your anger, and give you time to think.

After my initial meeting with Tony Robbins, I spent
the next few years researching how our external projections
influence our internal state. What I found was that every
aspect of life—be it attracting lovers, making money, getting
in shape, making new friends, connecting with family—is
directly connected to how we carry ourselves physically.

The Man Who Didn't Want to Disappear

One day, a client flew in from halfway across the globe to
see me.

I was just finishing up a phone call when my other
line lit up. "Sean," said my receptionist, "your client is here
to see you."

"Thanks, Carol, I'll be right out."

I reached for my blazer, brushed off every visible speck of lint I could find, and began the maneuvering process it takes me to get my jacket on by myself. I took a quick look at myself in the mirror to make sure nothing was out of place. I always want to make a strong impression on the client in the first few seconds of our initial meeting. I opened the door and rolled quickly down my office hallway to the waiting area. I was very curious. This client had written to me that he was in a very bad way and had been saving up for two years just to fly to Chicago to work with me.

As I rounded the corner, I saw him—I could tell by his scared expression and the defeated posture of his body. I'd seen this hundreds of times before in my clients and audience members. Clearly, he saw himself as broken and flawed. I saw him as a classic car or historic building with an unbelievable amount of potential for restoration.

"Thanks for coming!" I said. I gave him a giant smile and put a bounce of enthusiasm in my voice.

"Oh . . . well, you're welcome." His voice was barely audible.

As I led him down the hall to my office, I paid close attention to his physiology. He reminded me of Eeyore, from *Winnie the Pooh*. It wouldn't have shocked me if he'd said, "Have you seen my tail, Sean? Oh, poor me." His subzero self-esteem and lack of self-confidence were actually painful to look at. I knew I needed to act fast. His self-worth was sliding into an abyss as I watched.

In our e-mail correspondence, he had told me that he was in his late fifties and had never even kissed a girl. He thought he was coming to see me to work on his charisma with women, but that wasn't the case. It's never the case. When clients pay the money, take the time off from work, and travel to see me, we rarely work on the issue they thought that they had in the beginning.

This would be an intense, twelve-hour session. As we entered my office, he did what almost every client does: stop to take in the view. It was late in the afternoon, and the picture windows framed the most gorgeous sunset. Then he sank down into my soft and inviting brown couch, and we went to work. My number-one objective was to shift his physiology immediately. If I could get him to embrace his physical confidence, he would feel an instant upgrade in his outlook.

It was then that the words of Tony Robbins came bubbling up in my mind: "Motion creates Emotion!" I shared the whole concept of physical confidence with my client, and recommended that he begin by taking up as much space on the couch as he could. Self-consciously, he unfolded himself a bit. Then I began tweaking his body posture.

"Stretch your arms out," I said. As soon as he did this, he allowed his chest to open. Because it was no longer constricted by his bent-over, body-clutching posture, he was able to breathe freely and easily—maybe for the first time in years. And as soon as he stretched his arms to either side, and his chest expanded with healthy breaths, he automatically took up more space in the room. He seemed larger, and he felt larger to himself. He looked shocked for a moment, but right away—maybe in spite of himself—he began to relax.

I wanted to build on this, right away. "Lean back and uncross your legs," I instructed him. He became even more relaxed, and I could see just the smallest bit of confidence growing as he assumed the posture of a confident man.

"How do you feel now?" I asked.

"Better," he said, in a tiny voice.

"What? You'll have to speak up." I then got this extremely soft-spoken man to speak as loud as he could without yelling. Bit by bit, just by changing the way he sat, moved, breathed, and projected his voice, he had already begun a transformation to the person he really was. Time to go to another level.

"Have you ever heard of Milton H. Erickson?" I asked.

"Um, no, I don't think so."

"Dr. Erickson was a medical doctor and one of the greatest psychotherapists who ever lived. He had a way with people, a way to help them grow strong, like a tree. He taught men to plant their energy deep into the ground and feel the power of the earth in every cell of their being."

Now, I'm not sure if Dr. Erickson ever used this exact metaphor. During my PhD courses, however, I had studied hundreds of pages of his work. They all said the same thing, in just a slightly different way: get the client back in rapport with himself. This man was visibly out of rapport with himself, and I used the work of Erickson to drive home the point that he needed to be more grounded and centered in his power. It seemed to strike a chord deep within him.

As I watched, he straightened up his posture, placed both feet flat on the floor, and gently squinted his eyes. He seemed more grounded already, and it was magnificent to see.

As the session progressed, we worked on teaching him to stand, sit, walk, talk, and breathe like a man who owns his spot on the earth. I even took him to my underground parking garage and made him roar like a lion at the top of his lungs to awaken the primal animal he had locked away inside of him. By the time we broke for dinner, and he wheeled my wheelchair across the parking lot to the restaurant, I felt I was with a different person from the one who had walked in just a few hours earlier.

But really, what had I done? I merely helped him shift his body out of a space of physical insecurity and into a space of physical confidence. You'd swear miracles had been performed on this man. Truthfully, though, all he needed were two things:

1. Permission to be a man and own his place on the earth
2. The understanding of how it felt to embody physical confidence

By keeping up this practice every day—allowing his body to take up the space in the world that he really deserved—he reminded himself that he *was* a confident person. And others knew at first glance that it was true.

Viewing his transformation was truly breathtaking. But it's not only men who can be transformed by making changes in how they carry themselves.

The Woman Who Was Tired of Being Tired

The buzzing telephone jolted me out of my concentration. I was working hard to make a deadline for this book, and I was hunkered down in my office, writing this chapter. I'd told my receptionist to hold all my calls, and I figured she was just calling to say she was leaving for the night.

"Sean, you have a phone call. I know you're writing, but this client insists it's urgent. I didn't want to turn her away."

"Okay, fine, patch it through." I was annoyed. I just wanted to get back to my writing.

"How can I help you?" I began. The woman on the other end of the line sounded like a tightly wound spring. Her voice quality was distant, emotionally vacant. She wanted me to give her all my credentials, board certification details, and client testimonial letters. When new clients begin with these demands, it's often a sign that they have had a very bad previous experience with a therapist. I interrupted her volley of questions.

"I'm happy to share all those things and more with you," I said. "First, though, can you tell me why this call is so urgent?"

"I haven't slept in over forty-eight hours," she said. She was desperate. She also confirmed my original guess—she had been sexually abused by a therapist. "I'm really afraid that

I'll be psychologically damaged forever," she said, breaking
down in tears.

"Please," she said, "I need to come in for a session
immediately."

"Okay," I said, looking at the clock. It was just 4:59 PM.
Maybe I'd have time to write later. "I'll clear my schedule this
evening. Come on in."

She arrived at my office with a female friend, who
was there to drive her home afterward. Her body language was screaming, "HELP ME!" Her eyes were bugging
out of her head. Her body was as rigid as a board, and she
laughed shrilly every few minutes, for no reason and without warning. She made no eye contact. She reminded me of
an abandoned child wandering the world, fearful of everything. When she sat down, she tucked in her entire body so
as to take up as little space as possible on this planet, a very
common posture I'd noticed in abused women.

Right away, we went to work on her physiology, relaxing her body one muscle group at a time.

"Okay, imagine for a moment that you could relax all
the muscles around your eyes . . . good. Now relax your
cheeks. Relax your forehead."

Over the course of several minutes, I had her visualize
relaxing close to twenty-five major and minor muscle groups.
Then we talked about what she loved most on the planet
(gardening, her child, and cooking), and her face got softer
and less tense with these thoughts. Next, we concentrated on
deep breathing and creating a gentle smile.

I then told her to mirror my physiology exactly. I got into a very comfortable and confident physical position, head up and shoulders back. She had to follow suit and put her face, hands, arms, and legs into the exact same position, as if she were looking in a mirror. This activity creates a positive transference of emotion. In fact, if a person does this with enough attention to physical detail, she can sometimes even read the thoughts of the other person to some degree. I know that sounds a little spooky, but remember: your external state communicates your internal state. If you get into someone else's precise physical position, sometimes you can feel what he is feeling and thinking.

At the end of two hours of hard work, using these and other simple but powerful techniques to allow her body and mind to experience a new way of being in the world, the changes in her emotional attitude became apparent. Her tense muscles had finally let go, and her body was relaxed and softened. She was beginning to make steady eye contact with me, rather than darting her glance wildly around the room looking for danger. When she spoke, her voice was more modulated and under control. As she left my office that night, I was grateful that her friend was driving her home, because she was yawning, smiling, and slinking like a limp noodle to her car. The next morning, she left me a voice mail thanking me profusely for a great night of sleep.

If you can shift the body, you can shift the mind.

Slowwwwww ... Downnnnnn ...

One thing I hear over and over from clients is that they just don't have enough time. That's kind of funny, because our world moves fast, and we move fast—you'd think we'd have plenty of time. But moving fast makes us feel as if we can't catch up. Rushing certainly doesn't give us physical confidence. When we're running at top speed all the time, we can't relax, and others can't relax around us.

The solution is easy: Slow. Down. Your. Movements.

I'm not talking about moving as if you were running in slow motion; I am simply suggesting that you be more aware of how your body is moving. If you want to be more comfortable with yourself and make others feel comfortable when they are around you, pay attention to the following areas:

- **Relax.** Keep your entire body loose. If your fists are clenched, release them. Let go of any tension you're harboring anywhere in your body.
- **Breathe.** If you're taking shallow breaths, begin taking slower and deeper breaths. Be sure to exhale completely! If you find yourself fidgeting (for example, dipping your hands in and out of your pockets; fiddling with any object obsessively; chewing your nails; playing with your hair; tapping your feet, hands, or fingers), take a deep breath in, smile, gently place your body in a comfortable position—and leave it there.

- **Slow down your blinking.** Be aware of your blinking rate. If it's too fast, slow it down.

- **Bring your head up.** Keep your shoulders back and your head up. This will almost automatically keep your optimism up. When we look out at the world, we think about things outside ourselves. When we look down, we tend to go inward. Our mind accesses self-talk and emotions, and that can disconnect us from the present moment. Keeping your shoulders back will also open up your heart chakra and show others that you're open to giving and receiving love.

- **Adopt good posture.** Keep your body relaxed and slightly asymmetric. No sitting or standing at attention, with shoulders squared and feet together, like a soldier. This symmetric posture conveys the message that you're ready to attack, whereas holding your body slightly (yet consciously) off kilter conveys you have no intention to cause harm. You're just there to relax and have a good time.

- **Use a strong tone of voice.** Keep your voice under conscious control. If you listen to any good radio DJ, you'll notice that he never speaks in a slow, boring monotone. He keeps the volume, tempo, and pitch of his voice smooth and controlled. When he takes breaths, he makes the sound intentional.

- **Smile!** Please don't force a big, scary, stiff smile that stays plastered on your face no matter what. Make it a gentle, subtle smile that comes from your open heart and feels comfortable.

- **Be peaceful.** The more still and calm you are, the better. Our eyes and ears catch sudden or awkward changes in movements and sounds, and automatically register them as potential threats. The more you can keep your body still and your voice controlled and relaxed, the better equipped you'll be to keep the peace around you and certainly within you.

Sensory Acuity

If you pay close attention to microchanges in physiology, you can tell when your feelings (or someone else's feelings) are shifting. Our awareness of these details is referred to as *sensory acuity*. The following physical cues telegraph your internal emotional condition:

- **Pupil dilation:** The larger the pupils, the more open and connected we feel (if not influenced by direct light or drugs, that is).
- **Flushed skin:** The more red the skin (specifically in the face), the more uncomfortable, fearful, embarrassed, or sexually nervous we feel.
- **Muscle tension:** The tenser the facial muscles, specifically around the eyes, the more uncomfortable we are. Neck tension is a very good indicator of feeling overwhelmed.
- **Quick breathing:** The more quickly we breathe (unless we have just done some physical activity), the shallower the

breaths we take, and the higher in the lungs our breath comes from, the more constricted we feel (and probably are) overall. If we take slow, deep, and full belly breaths, we're likely to be more comfortable in the moment.

- **Lip configuration:** If our lips are unnaturally pursed and slightly white, we're likely to be upset or extremely displeased. If the lips are full, smooth, and a deep shade of red, we may be feeling sexually aroused, emotionally excited, or at total peace.

GET OFF YOUR BUT *NOW!*
Reading Body Language

Ready to sharpen your sensory acuity?

First, ask one of your friends if she'll take part in a harmless psychological experiment. Then tell her to visualize a person she can't stand, and to hold that image in her mind for one solid minute. Watch as she does this, observing the microchanges listed previously (pupils, skin, muscles, breathing, lips). When the minute is up, have her recite her telephone number to you backwards. This will clear her brain.

Now have her visualize someone she admires, holding that image in her mind for one minute. Again, observe the microchanges. They should be very different. When the minute is up, have her clear her mind again by counting the number of letters in her full name.

Finally, ask her to think about someone she either loves or hates—without telling you which one she picked—and think about that person for one minute. Observe the microchanges, and see if you can intuit the answer simply by using your sensory acuity. No matter how much of a poker face your friend may claim to have, your sensory acuity should still be able to crack the case.

Finding Romance Through Physical Confidence

Men and women often misunderstand how sexual attraction works. They think all that matters is their height, their weight, their body shape, and the appearance of their face and hair. Those attributes certainly play a role in getting our attention, yet they are nowhere near as influential in our selection process as physical confidence.

Here's an example. Let's say a tall, dark, and handsome chap enters a bar with a scowl on his face; he looks down at his feet, has his arms folded, and makes jerky movements with his arms, legs, and torso. How many women do you think he'll attract? None! Women will rule him out on first visual contact, labeling him as creepy, weird, and possibly dangerous. Why? This guy is projecting physical insecurity.

Conversely, if a short, plump, and barely decent-looking fellow comes into that same bar projecting a playful, genuine, and powerful physical confidence, he will dramatically improve his chances of pairing off with the woman of his choosing.

What about women? Women who attract emotionally unhealthy and unstable men often do so because of their body language. Some of these guys can easily zero in on a woman they can manipulate, use, and abuse. How do they do it? Simple. They overlook all the women in the place who project authentic physical confidence, and look for those who project physical insecurity: the ones who are twitchy and stiff, who won't smile or make eye contact. These mannerisms are homing beacons to emotionally unstable men.

When we project physical confidence—whether we are men or women—we can't help but attract high-caliber people. Time and time again, a woman will catch my eye from clear across a crowded room. Usually, she will not be the "hottest" girl in the place, at least by media standards. But invariably, her physical confidence will be off the charts. A woman like this is comfortable in her own body; her warm smile and direct eye contact say, "I'm loving life!" This kind of physical confidence is absolutely compelling. I almost always make an effort to connect with these women—and more often than not, that connection leads to a relationship.

I get e-mails on a daily basis from people who complain, "Sean, I would approach more women and have a better dating life, BUT I don't look like . . . [insert movie star name]."

This comment always makes me want to laugh. I'm often tempted to scream at them, "Then how do you explain my great dating life? I'm only three feet tall and use a wheelchair. These are not hot selling points in the dating world. It's my attitude and my physical confidence that attract women."

How do I know this? The women I go out with tell me! "Sean, you have an extremely commanding presence. Every single movement you make is with purpose, and that is *hot!*"

This is no accident. It took me years to learn this, and now I put it into practice every day. *Anyone reading this book can implement the same principles that I've learned.* I don't hold any magical powers that are off-limits to anyone else.

One more story. A few months ago I was in a coffee shop writing an article for my men's online magazine when two women about twenty years my senior came in together. One woman was quite natural—the lines around her mouth and eyes gave her age away. I found her attractive, even though she was much older than I. The other woman was a different story. Apparently, her plastic surgeon had run a sale, and she'd gotten every procedure possible. Her body was sculpted to "perfection," and she did indeed look younger—albeit artificially—than her all-natural counterpart, yet I felt no sexual attraction toward her. Why?

The all-natural woman projected a youthful spirit. She glided across the room, filled with vitality. The other woman looked like a stiff branch that had snapped off a tree. If you want to be seen as sexy, you must project a vital, fluid physical confidence.

Burst Through Any Challenge

I've worked with all sorts of athletes, from high school and NCAA to professional and Olympic. Over and over again, at every level of competition, I've seen *physical confidence* determine the outcome of the game. When you walk onto a court or a field—chest puffed out, head held high, and wearing a cocksure grin—you will almost always take home a prize. The same is true for the Fortune 500 executives I've worked with. Those who are conscious of their movements and in control of their breathing and posture keep their cool no matter what happens.

Fortunately, you don't have to be a world-class athlete or wealthy CEO to express physical confidence in your life. The next time you find yourself faced with a major challenge and your body shrinks into a physical space of insecurity, *stop*. Roll your shoulders back, breathe deeply, and keep your chin up. Show the world that you mean business, and you will even convince yourself.

GET OFF YOUR BUT *NOW!*
Put Your Body in the Confidence Zone

This is a great activity to try when you're nervous about a big meeting, a romantic date, or a difficult conversation.

Step 1: Play your favorite song over and over while looking in a mirror.

Step 2: Stand tall, with your legs a few feet apart.

Step 3: Put your hands at your side, like Superman or Wonder Woman.

Step 4: Squint or widen your eyes, depending on whichever makes you feel tougher.

Step 5: Put a cocksure smile on your face and slowly nod your head yes.

Step 6: Feel the confident energy coursing through your veins. Create a physical reminder of that emotional experience (for example, lightly squeeze both fists, squeeze your thumbs and forefingers together, tap your nose once, whatever). This will create a "kinesthetic anchor"—a movement that will fire off the feeling you want to evoke.

Step 7: Once you arrive at your meeting, date, or conversation, trigger the kinesthetic anchor.

Step 8: Experience the confident feelings that flood your entire body. Enjoy the moment—you are receiving the power and support you need.

By now, you should have more than enough evidence to be convinced that how you feel is determined by what you say to yourself and how you carry yourself physically. Yet no matter how great your self-talk and how confident your stance, you can be thrown off balance in less than a second if you don't control what you focus your attention on.

Our next lesson is all about how to manage and control your focus, what you need to focus on, and what you should *never* focus on. For now, you can just focus on reading the next chapter.

Note

1. www.caremark.com/wps/portal/HEALTH_RESOURCES?
   topic=mindbodygut

HOW ANDRÉA GOT OFF HER BUT

"I'm overweight, BUT it's not my fault."

Developing your physical confidence is going to do wonders for how you feel about yourself each day and how people treat you. The catch, though, is that if you're not *already* in good shape, it will be a struggle to maintain your physical confidence. This is because aches, pains, exhaustion, and being overweight are drains on the psyche that can actually inhibit feelings of self-worth. When you are shamed and blamed on top of it, it's easy for your BUTS to weigh you down.

Sadly, being out of shape is a problem that the majority of our society is battling. That's why I am so impressed with my dear friend Andréa.

She calls me her "Soul Brotha" because she believes (as do I) that we share cosmic DNA. An interesting phenomenon always takes place when we go out in public together. People honestly don't know whom to stare at: the little guy in the wheelchair or the hot blonde with the energy of a rocket ship. What these onlookers would never guess is that even though Andréa looks like a show-stopping model now, she wasn't always a picture of vibrant health. Far from it.

Like me, one of the challenges she faced in her life had to do with overcoming something she was born with: in her case, it was so-called fat genes that cause her to gain weight and store fat extremely easily. No matter how much she dieted, she always gained the weight back. If you live in the United States, there's a 60 percent chance that you've struggled with this too.

For most of her life, Andréa heard two opposing messages. Doctors and scientists explained, "It's your genetics that are making you fat. There's nothing you can do about it." She had the message "BUT I can't do anything about my weight" embedded in her mind from a very early age. On the opposite side of the fence, the multibillion-dollar health industry screamed from magazines and billboards that if she bought their products and programs, she would lose weight fast! So her choice was either to resign herself to obesity or to fail repeatedly at losing weight and learn to think of herself as a failure with no willpower.

She didn't get a lot of encouragement, from others or from her own experiences. She had dieted her way through college, but graduated even heavier than when she started. She would lose some weight for a few months, but it would always come back. She fell in love with a man while she was in a thin phase, and really thought he was the one. But he rejected her when she began gaining back the weight. And then it got even worse . . . He blamed her for not having the "willpower" to lose weight. She promised to lose the weight, but when it didn't happen fast enough for

Andréa's boyfriend, he decided to do something about it. One day while they were at the beach, he pulled out a camera and told her to stand there without "sucking in" (as she normally would) because he wanted her to see how much weight she had gained. She was humiliated and embarrassed, but worst of all, she was disgusted with herself and how she looked.

Like so many others in her position, she went through a dark period, becoming addicted to diet pills and seriously considering getting surgery to cut away parts of her body. By this time she *hated* her body, blaming it for her unhappiness as if it were separate from herself. Andréa had a million BUTS disguised as "reasons" for why she would never be able to have the healthy, radiant, fat-free body that she desired:

BUT I can't afford to eat healthy food and get a fitness trainer . . .

BUT food makes me feel so good when I'm bored, upset, or lonely . . .

BUT my genetics make me fat . . .

Every day and every moment, she battled her BUTS.

Now here's the reason that Andréa says she and I share the same cosmic DNA: like me, she didn't give up. In struggling with her BUTS, she slowly but surely learned that she could *tune them out*. She didn't listen to them! Even though she seemed to be the only one who believed she could fight against her genetics and her culture, she kept trying and kept searching for the answer.

I talk a lot about the mind-body connection in this book. Andréa made a slightly different discovery. She awakened to the fact that she wasn't just her body: she also had a spirit. When she realized that her spirit and body were *connected*, she began to see herself in a new light. Before, she had seen only fat and disappointment. Now she began to see the beauty of her *self*. And here's the amazing part: she began to lose weight, without even trying. As the outside of her body began to reflect the love she was feeling on the inside, she took on a new, radiant glow of inner joy.

This may seem magical; many epiphanies do. But in reality her transformation was the result of years of struggling, searching for answers, and systematically eliminating unworkable weight-loss plans. Over the months and years that followed, the voice of her genetic BUT faded away. She went from a size 12 (getting bigger and bigger every year) to a size 2, and is becoming healthier and more fit every year.

Andréa no longer considers herself "cursed" by her fat genes. In fact, she considers those genes a blessing, because it was her weight that got her to focus on something that she might have otherwise neglected: her health.

"I stopped focusing on losing weight," she told me, "and I started focusing on *gaining* health!"

Today she is a radio show host, author, and public speaker. She has helped thousands of women and men around the world turn off their "fat genes" and lose weight without going to war with their bodies. How? By inspiring them to get off their BUTS, connect with their inner spirit, and start loving their bodies and lives.

Over the years, I've met hundreds of men and women who have struggled with their weight all their lives. Like Andréa, many of them believe they are cursed, unlucky, and unattractive. Unlike Andréa, they are still stuck on their BUTS.

If you've read Andréa's amazing story—and if you've seen how beautiful Andréa is today—you're probably thinking, "Sure, it was easy for her. Look at how hot she is!" But it took Andréa years of pain and struggle to arrive at her "overnight" transformation. She's no different from anyone else. She's no different from you.

So what does Andréa's story mean to you, if you're among the millions of men and women who lose weight over and over again, just to gain it back? Here's what I tell my clients:

You will continue to struggle with your weight if you blame others or shame yourself. Blame statements, such as, "I would exercise, BUT my boss keeps me too busy," and shame statements, such as "I would be in shape, BUT I'm a lazy pig," will do nothing to help you change your life. These statements only breed discouragement.

After so many years, it's no surprise that when you look in the mirror, all you can see is fat. It's time for you to look *beyond* the fat, right into your soul. You'll see something right away: you really *are* no different than Andréa. Your "self" is attractive—it is just waiting for you to acknowledge it and ask for support. Allow your spirit, mind, and body to work together to help you create an amazing new body, the one that was there all along.

LESSON 4

Focus Your Focus

The ability to manage your focus is one of your greatest powers. What you put your attention on determines what you accomplish, how you feel, and what you can handle in life. You might even say that it has the biggest influence over what happens to you in life. Here's the perfect example . . .

Happiness Is Right in Front of You

When I gripped the wheels on my wheelchair that summer afternoon in 2002, I thought I was headed for a brief roll through the park for some fresh air and mild exercise. As it turned out, I was actually setting out on one of the most life-altering days I've ever experienced.

I travel quite a bit for my speaking career, spending literally hundreds of hours crammed in confined spaces with people who are often cranky, tired, and angry at the world.

I cherish my time at home, and love taking leisurely rolls in the park behind my house. Usually a family member, friend, or love interest joins me on these jaunts, pushing my wheelchair or walking alongside me as we share conversation. This day, for some reason, I decided to go it alone.

As I wheeled down my driveway and rounded the bend toward the park, I saw a house I'd never seen before. It looked as if it had just been built, and it was gorgeous— probably three times the size of mine.

To make it even more perfect, the house was overflowing with life. The family dog was running up and down the length of the front yard, and a young brother and sister were giggling as they played fetch with the pup. In the large kitchen window, I could see their mother and father preparing dinner. It was as though a Norman Rockwell painting had come to life on my street. Everything seemed in perfect harmony for them, yet this lovely scene sent my mood plummeting. I went from enjoying the day to feeling empty inside, and I was gripped by one consuming thought: "I'll be happy when I get to live in a house that large."

Why didn't I have what my neighbors had? I wanted a bigger home! If I had a bigger home, then my neighbors would see that I had become something, I had made something of my life. Yet I was still living in the home I grew up in as a child. To the outside world, I must look like a failure. As I continued down the path into the park, I felt overwhelmingly discouraged.

Suddenly, I was jolted into the present by the purring engine noise that unmistakably announces my favorite piece of machinery—a Porsche. I looked up and down the road just to catch a glimpse of it. There it was, shining red in the late afternoon light. My heart raced. What would it be like to step on the gas pedal, forced back into my leather bucket seat by the speed of acceleration?

Just the thought of owning such a car brought me soaring—though temporary—elation. I imagined what it would be like to roll up to my friends' houses and honk the horn. The looks on their faces when they saw me in a bright red Porsche would be worth as much as the car.

Then the driver sped off, taking my feelings of happiness along with the car. I hated the boring vehicle sitting in the driveway of my everyday boring house. I wanted more. I couldn't be happy until I had it.

I wheeled on. By this time, the sun was setting. I had almost reached the other side of the park when I experienced a third glaring reminder of how much my life was lacking. A young woman close to my age came jogging directly toward me on the path. As she drew closer, my heart stopped. She was beautiful. Her body was flawless. Everything about her moved with grace and ease as she rapidly neared me. This girl was what I call "amnesia hot"—so hot I couldn't even remember my own name in her presence. Our eyes met briefly. We shared a split second together. The smell of her soft perfume filled my nose as she ran past. I was in heaven.

I thought, "I'll be so happy when I'm dating a girl like that." Then my train of thought derailed, crashing into a series of discouraging questions that repeated in an endless loop.

"Why don't you have a girlfriend like that, Sean?"

"Why aren't you married yet?"

"How come you haven't been able to afford that Porsche?

"Why don't you live in that big, new house?"

The more I tried to avoid these negative thoughts, the faster my mind raced down this dark path. When I'd set out an hour or so ago, I was feeling pretty good. Now I couldn't believe how discontented I felt with my life.

By this time, I'd reached the end of the park, and the sky was growing as dark as my mind. At that moment, an inner light bulb went on. I had *completely* missed the point of my roll through the park.

The reason I'd gone to the park in the first place was to unwind, be with nature, and get some exercise. Instead, I'd turned into a tense ball of despair, focusing all my energy on what was lacking in my life. I was so busy focusing on all the things I didn't have that I overlooked everything I did have. I took a deep breath, looked around, and started over.

It was a glorious day. Or at least it had been when I'd started. The weather couldn't have been more perfect. The flowers were in full bloom—yellows and reds and oranges and purples—and I had wheeled right past them, obsessed with my lack of stuff. But was I really lacking so much?

Even though I might not have had the largest home in the neighborhood, at least I lived in a safe neighborhood. I might not have had the fastest or newest car, but it worked just fine at hauling me around from place to place. As for the hot girlfriend, I was simply being impatient. When the right girl comes along it will be meant to be. Unfortunately, I had focused so hard on everything that I didn't have, I had forgotten about the greatest thing I did have: my life. I was right here, right now.

Suddenly, I flashed back to the day I spoke to a university class, and noticed an empty chair in the front row. Later, the professor told me sadly that the young woman who should have been sitting there had died that morning in a freak accident at her dorm. I was shocked. She wasn't much younger than I was.

The time we are given here is fleeting. We think it's going to last forever, but it's not. We just never know when it's going to be our turn to go. I couldn't believe I'd wasted these precious life moments focusing on what I thought I was lacking!

With my focus readjusted from negative to positive, I sat at the end of the path in the park and looked back. Now I could smell the scent of flowers in the air, and the green leaves on the shady trees filled my eyes. Some dogs were barking in the neighborhood, and I could hear the laughter of kids running home for dinner. I began to focus on all we ever really have: the present. It really is a gift, a gift of time.

GET OFF YOUR BUT *NOW!*
Stop Searching for the Blue

Try this experiment with a friend.

Stand behind him and ask him to focus on everything in the room that's blue. Ask him to make a mental note of each blue item he can see in front of him. When he's done, ask him to close his eyes and tell you everything in the room he remembers seeing that was the color yellow (or any other color that isn't blue). More than likely, he'll laugh and say, "I can't!"

That's because his brain spent all its conscious energy focusing exclusively on blue. It labeled all the other colors as insignificant and didn't even see them.

That's how our minds work. Once we start looking exclusively for the blue, we have trouble finding any yellow. When we look for what we don't like or don't have, we see and remember only that.

How Focus Works

Our conscious mind can focus on only about seven chunks of data per second. After that, it loses focus. For example, when you're trying to drive, and you're also drinking coffee, reading a map, listening to the radio, talking on your cell phone, and checking yourself out in the rearview mirror, you can easily forget about the most important thing you're doing—driving—and you run the risk of crashing several tons of metal into a cement barrier or nearby tree. Even if you're not in a car, however, it's *never* a good idea to spread your focus too thin.

Think of your focus as the area that a small flashlight can illuminate in a dark room. There may be tons of things in the room, but you can see only what that beam of light is shining on. The same holds true with mental focus. There are an infinite number of things to pay attention to, yet our focus limits us to a relative few. And these few are of prime importance. As my close friend and mentor Zan Perrion has told me many times, "Whatever you focus on, your life will head in that direction."

His wisdom applies to every aspect of life. I've learned this firsthand from observing my clients. The happiest ones focus on all the great things in life, and the most miserable ones focus on all the things that are going wrong. In fact, I believe I have found a foolproof recipe for misery: focus on all the things you don't like and don't have in life, and don't think about anything else. It's that simple.

The Egg-Timer Technique

My parents never formally studied a word of psychology, yet they instinctively knew that if I focused too long on a negative aspect of my life, I would only make it worse. They also knew they couldn't deny me the experiences of sadness, anger, and self-pity, because I would merely repress the feelings and express them in some destructive way later. So they came up with an ingenious solution.

If they caught me feeling sorry for myself, they would say, "Sean, if you want to feel sorry for yourself, that's totally okay." They would then go to the kitchen, rustle around in the pantry, and return with an egg timer and this instruction: "However, Sean, today you only get fifteen minutes. Ready? *Go!*" And the egg timer would click off the minutes.

Of course, after five minutes of wallowing in uninterrupted self-pity, I would get bored and want to go play. They would then remind me that I had another ten minutes to go. This tactic allowed me to immerse myself in self-pity for a prescribed period of time instead of dragging it out over the course of days, weeks, or a lifetime. This taught me to focus like a laser and then move on.

Mom and Dad made the constraints of self-pity very clear: "Sean," they told me, "you can certainly cry if you want to. You're just not allowed to drown in your tears."

Eventually, this trained my brain to see pity as useless and ineffective. As I grew older, my moments of self-pity grew less and less common.

I remember a conversation my dad and I had during one of my fifteen-minute pity parties when I was about nine or ten. I was mad because all my buddies were able to play basketball, while I had to sit on the sidelines and could only watch. I was focusing on what I couldn't do, which of course felt horrible. Here's how my father handled it.

"Sean," he said, "focus on what you *can* do and what you *do* have in your life. You may not be able to play in the NBA, but if you spend your energy getting wealthy, someday you can *own* an NBA team!"

All these years later, I've never forgotten that conversation. It was an "Aha!" moment that taught me the importance of controlling my focus. My mom and dad had hundreds of talks with me when I was a kid about the power of focusing on what I had instead of what I didn't have. Years later, I realized they were really teaching me the power of gratitude. Gratitude is simply focused appreciation. It is nearly impossible to be upset in a space of gratitude.

GET OFF YOUR BUT *NOW!*
Focus on What You Have

Think about it: you have so much more than you have probably ever realized. Take out your Get Off Your BUT Now! journal and write down twenty-five things you have acquired, have control over, or were fortunate enough to be born with (for example, the ability to read this book).

If you really want to take this activity to the next level, leave this list next to your bed and casually read it from time to time. Read it whenever you're feeling discouraged, to remind yourself of what's great about you and your life.

Compare Leads to Despair

In the park that day, I was miserable because I was focusing on what I lacked instead of what I had. I just kept thinking that everyone else had so much *more.* Comparing ourselves to others is a game that ends badly no matter which way you play it. If you act as if you're worse off than others, you will believe it, and you will live your life feeling inferior. If you act as if you're superior to others, you'll believe that too—and you'll live a life of arrogance; no one will want to be around you. This little mantra says it all: "Compare leads to despair."

Anytime I catch myself feeling sad because I don't have something someone else does, I repeat my mantra, and the gnawing feeling of lacking something quickly subsides. This happens because I'm deliberately shifting my focus off of what I don't have and on to what I do have.

Be a Rain Runner

It's fascinating how much time, money, and energy we spend trying to have more and be better than others. I wonder how much stuff is bought in our society for the sole purpose of looking better than our neighbors. We look over our shoulders constantly, focusing on what others think of us—and it's a never-ending drain on our energy reserves. Here's a case in point.

A few years ago, when I was twenty-five, I asked a girl out to a movie and dinner afterward, at a café across the street from the theater. When the movie let out, we headed to the front doors of the theater. It was pouring down rain. And not just any kind of rain. We're talking about *big fat Forrest Gump rain!*

I smiled at her and said, "You ready?"

"NO!"

"Why not?" I couldn't figure out what the problem was. All we had to do to get to the café was make a quick dash across the street.

"Sean," she said, frowning, "we don't have an umbrella!"

"So what?"

"If we go out there, we're going to get wet."

"And . . . ?" I said in confusion.

"If we get wet, then my hair is going to get wet!" She gave a shudder of horror.

"So what's the big deal about that?"

Now she was tapping her foot and rolling her eyes. "Sean, if my hair gets wet, then, well . . . people are going to stare at me." Case closed.

I paused, momentarily stunned, then I replied, "Sweetheart, you'll be standing next to a three-foot-tall twenty-five-year-old man in a wheelchair. They ain't gonna be looking at *you!*"

"I'm not doing it." She was adamant.

At this point, my frustration had risen to a nearly uncontrollable level. I took a deep breath. "Okay, time out. Let's imagine twenty-five years have gone by, and we're not even in each other's lives anymore, but we think back about this date we went on where it was pouring down rain and we went running through that rain together. We remember that we stopped and looked deep into each other's eyes. Wouldn't that be a memory you'd be willing to create *right now?*"

A few seconds passed as she gave this romantic idea some thought. Then she shook her head firmly. "No! I just can't stand the thought of people looking at me with my hair all ruined."

I felt so shot down. That was the smoothest material I had ever used on a girl, and it had failed miserably. Or had it? After further review, I realized that this was surely not the girl for me. I wanted to date women who were willing to run in the rain, literally and metaphorically. From that moment on, I was determined to surround myself not only with women but also with business partners and friends who were willing to be rain runners.

To take a chance on happiness and adventure is a way to build your dreams. To focus on *not* doing something because of what others might think of you is a way to completely lose touch with your authentic self.

Laughing at Stress

When we constantly focus on what others think of us (more correctly, what we *think* others think of us), we make every decision in a space of hesitation and fear. This focus on what we're afraid of causes the body to live in a constant state of panic, stressing all its systems. Some amount of stress is fine, and inevitable in life. But this constant stress causes more illnesses and premature deaths than can ever be recorded.

The remedies for stress are legion: yoga, music, meditation, interpretive dance, jogging, reading, deep breathing, you name it. It can be stressful just trying to pick a stress reliever! Fortunately, my personal remedy for stress relief requires no training and can be done anywhere, at any time, by anyone. What is it?

Laughter.

The benefits of laughter are impressive. It boosts your immune system, exercises practically every muscle group, and releases natural pain-relieving chemicals into your bloodstream. Even a small amount of research into laughter yields an overwhelming amount of evidence that laughter heals. In fact, even curving your mouth upward in the semblance of a smile—no matter how you feel inside—stimulates your brain to release healing chemicals into your system.

What is there to laugh about? Good question. I'd guess that if you're reading this book right now, you feel under some kind of pressure—to finish the job; get things done; solve your problems; change and improve your life; stay ahead of bills, taxes, and societal expectations. I'm no exception. Yet when I find myself starting to slip into this trap, I've learned to focus my focus on one solitary question: "What's funny about this?" This puts all my conscious awareness on seeing the comical side of any situation, and the resulting laughter takes care of the stress.

My elevator story illustrates a worst-case-scenario version of this technique that I think you'll remember for a long time . . .

How to Get Unstuck

One July morning in 1998, when I was working for Congressman William O. Lipinski on Capitol Hill, I had arrived at work early and was looking forward to sipping my piping hot tea and reading the daily paper at my desk before my coworkers arrived. Unfortunately, when I showed up, my boss had already arrived and was seated at his desk—he'd come in early to get ready for a morning meeting. There went my tea and paper.

"Sean," he said, "normally, I'd ask someone else on staff to run this note over to the other side of the building, but you're the only one in. Do you think you could manage to get this out right now?"

I had explored the Longworth building fairly well by this time, so I knew pretty much every corner of the place. "That shouldn't be a problem, Congressman."

"Great!" Without taking his eyes off the stack of notes he was reviewing, he handed me an envelope.

I grabbed the letter from him, arranged my tea and paper in my chair, and set out on my early morning excursion.

When I got to the other side of the empty building, I found myself at a bank of elevators I had never taken before. Because my arms aren't as long as most people's, I carry a wooden stick in my wheelchair to help me push the elevator buttons. I pressed the button to call the elevator; it came immediately. I rolled in, and the doors closed. So far so good. Then I used my stick to push the button for the floor I was headed to.

Nothing happened.

I made several more attempts, pressing harder and harder with each one. Again, nothing.

These buttons must be heat sensitive! They wanted body heat from a finger, and all I had was this wooden stick. Great. I was stuck in a working elevator.

That's when I got creative. *What would MacGyver do?* I thought. The answer came to me in an instant: heat up the stick with my breath. I blew and blew until I figured it was warm enough, and pressed the button again.

Nothing!

The only thing heating up was my temper. I began mumbling obscenities under my breath and shaking my head from side to side. "This is RIDICULOUS!!" I shouted to the Elevator Gods. Then I thought, *What would Mom do if she was stuck in my position?* I could hear her voice: "Pretend the stick is a thermometer and take your temperature under your armpit with it."

I ran the stick into my shirt and began warming it up between my arm and torso. I rubbed it back and forth to create more heat through friction. Finally, I quickly whipped the stick out from under my shirt and pressed the button.

Nothing.

By this time I was furious. I knew yelling and pounding on the door would be useless—no one would hear me for at least another forty-five minutes, when the offices would begin opening for the day. I couldn't even press the security button to call for help.

I made one last-ditch effort to heat up my stick by sitting on it. Maybe the weight of my body would be enough to heat it up. I shoved the stick between my legs and ground out enough friction to practically start a fire. "Who's your daddy!" I yelled, knowing no one would hear me. Had this scene been caught on camera, I'm sure I would have been arrested for indecency in an elevator! I pulled the stick out and pressed the button for the fourth and final time.

Nothing.

It's not fair! I thought. *I'm stuck in this elevator just because my arms are too short to reach the buttons! No one else would have this problem! I must be the first person on the face of the earth to be trapped in a working elevator.* And then I burst out laughing.

As I laughed harder and harder, I noticed my stress levels plummeting. My overall feeling of well-being skyrocketed. What was the big deal? I knew I wasn't in any grave danger. Eventually someone would call the elevator from the outside, and I would be able to get off safely. The congressman wouldn't fire me because I couldn't press the elevator button. I just had to wait it out until someone used the elevator.

So I scooted my wheelchair up to one of the side walls and leaned against it, reading my paper and enjoying my tea. Just what I had wanted to do before I set off on this errand.

Another half hour passed. By this time, the elevator had become my home away from home. I'd read almost the entire paper, tossing each section on the elevator floor when I'd finished. Clearly, I'd settled in nicely by this time.

And then the elevator finally shook from its slumber.

The doors opened, a man stepped in—and stopped in his tracks, staring in complete confusion. It was obvious he couldn't even begin to make sense out of what he was seeing.

"How long have you been in here?" he asked finally, with great concern in his voice.

"Umm . . . well . . . I guess long enough to get to the sports section," I said with a smile. "Would you mind pressing the button for the third floor?"

I got off the elevator, delivered the congressman's letter, and then went straight to the building supervisor to inform him of the elevator debacle.

"How can I help you?" he said in a condescending voice.

"I'm here to report that you have an elevator trapping people who can't reach to activate the heat-sensitive buttons. I couldn't get my wooden elevator stick hot enough."

He looked up from his desk. "Boy," he said, "they aren't heat-sensitive buttons! They're activated by an electrical current your body naturally gives off. If you would have just had a little tinfoil at the end of your stick, you would have activated the sensor and been just fine."

I looked him square in the eyes and shouted, "Who comes to work with TINFOIL? It's not like I was expecting to bake a batch of brownies in the elevator!"

Then we both burst out laughing.

That's when I realized that laughter is one of my secret weapons against stress. Laughter has saved me from exploding into rage or weeping hysterically over the many challenges I've faced. Whether it's broken bones or being an elevator castaway, humor has helped me keep my wits about me all these years. The next time you find yourself in an unfair position, focus on what's funny about it.

Here's my prescription:

Giggle more.

Smile more.

Have a good belly laugh as often as possible!

GET OFF YOUR BUT *NOW!*
How to Lighten Up!

My clients are often weighted down by the plight of stress. When I feel that they need to lighten up, I give them this assignment.

1. Put a big, goofy grin (not a scary clown smile!) on your face.

2. Pull up the memory of one of the funniest things you've ever seen, heard, or experienced.

3. As you focus on your funny memory, increase the brightness of the picture—make it louder, bigger, and more lifelike in your mind. Pretend you are back in that moment and feel the uncontrollable laughter bubbling up inside you.

4. Pull up the memory of a time you laughed so hard you cried, or fell on the floor.

5. Breathe in that feeling of happiness and send it through your bloodstream.

6. Notice how much lighter your body feels.

7. Finish up by squeezing your nose!

Practice this activity several times over a few days. The next time you ever find yourself focusing on something sad, upsetting, or unfair, simply squeeze your nose. Feel all those moments of laughter flood your mind and wash out any unrest in your body.

Fairness Is an Illusion

One of the toughest parts of my job is helping people who can't stop focusing on what's not fair. I call it the "BUT it's not fair" disease. These people are complainers, and their complaints range from the pettiest ("BUT it's not fair that my Chihuahua can't come into this restaurant with me") to the most extreme ("BUT it's not fair that my parents died in a car accident and now I have to live in a foster home").

Rich, poor, it doesn't matter. Over the years, I've learned that anyone can be afflicted with this disease, from disadvantaged school kids to wealthy corporate executives. Whoever you are, the cure is the same. Be forewarned: it may feel uncomfortable at first. However, if you embrace it, I promise you it will set you free from your struggles. Ready? Here it is:

Fairness is an illusion.

Fairness never existed and never will.

No one in life gets less or more than anyone else. We just get different stuff.

That's right. No one is dealt a bad or a good hand in life; we're just dealt cards. It's up to us to stay in the game and play. Sure, some cards look "better," but they're really not. If you look closely, you'll see that anything you feel has been taken from you—or never given to you at all—was replaced with other amazing opportunities and gifts. It's up to you to find them.

At first glance, most people think I was dealt a bum hand in life. But it's not true. I've learned that I'm much stronger than people think—and much stronger than I once thought. The world is as open to me as it is to everyone else. In my opinion, I live the life of a rock star—and I wouldn't trade it for the world.

Just like yours, my body is what it is. I keep it in good shape, and I pump more enjoyment in and out of it than most people who have a more able body. I've stayed in the game, and I'm playing to win. You can too, no matter what cards you were dealt.

It all comes down to what you focus on. I focus on what's great about my life, and that puts me head and shoulders over the guy who looks like Brad Pitt but is too busy focusing on what's not fair about his life.

The next time you find yourself stressing out, look for what's funny in the situation instead of what's "not fair." You're holding a very powerful flashlight: your conscious awareness. Be very careful where you shine it, because that is what you will choose to focus on.

You and I are together on the path right now. Someday, we'll get to the end of our walk in the park. Until then, let's make sure we get everything we can out of life by focusing not on what we lack but on all the things we love and are grateful for.

One important thing for us to be grateful for is that we don't have to make this trip all by ourselves! We're fortunate to have the ability to bring other people into our lives. In our next lesson, I'm going to show you how to create a peer group that supports you every step of the way, fills your life with magical moments, empowers you when you're faced with your biggest BUTS—and helps you get off them!

HOW MIKE GOT OFF HIS BUT

"I would speak out about
sexual assault, BUT I'm not
an expert—no one would take
me seriously."

If you want to talk about someone who can focus his focus, my good friend Mike Domitrz is the perfect example. When he says he's going to do something, I never have a doubt that he will. I've had the fortunate pleasure of observing him closely over the years. It doesn't matter if he's with his kids at home, on stage educating a crowd, or behind the screen of his laptop—Mike is focused like a laser on the issue at hand. The more important reason that I admire him so much, and why I have chosen to bring his story into your life, is this: he always knows exactly *where* to put his focus.

Instead of scattering his energies when something goes wrong, he places his focus on the areas over which he has control. This skill has served him well, even in what he calls his darkest hour, back in 1989 when Mike was a college sophomore studying theatre. He returned to his residence hall one afternoon to find a note taped to his door: "Call home IMMEDIATELY!" He knew something was terribly wrong.

"Mike," his mom said in a shaky voice, "I have some bad news. Cheri has been raped." His sister had been raped! Mike began to cry, then he was filled with anger and rage. He wanted to kill the person who had done this to his sister.

He didn't act on that impulse, but the anger ate away at him. His entire worldview had been shot to pieces by his sister's rape. He'd always been a focused person, going after what he wanted, but now that focus was gone. He couldn't concentrate—his life seemed meaningless. Within one year of Cheri's assault, Mike went from being an honors student to almost being expelled for bad grades. He went from knowing exactly what he wanted in life to questioning *everything* in life. He searched for security and stability and found himself becoming unstable and insecure. He felt guilty for not having protected Cheri, even though he couldn't have.

Eventually, Mike transferred to the college in his hometown to be close to his sister and family. Soon the trial would begin, and the rapist would be convicted. That didn't make Mike feel much better, though. He was angry and frustrated. He still wanted to do something to help, BUT he was just a college kid. What could he possibly do? The more he told himself he couldn't do anything, the more helpless he felt. His inability do anything about what had happened to his sister was eating away at him.

Then, one afternoon, Mike and the other members of his college swim team were given a mandate to attend a sexual assault awareness course. He'd never come across such a thing before, and sitting through it was like getting an electric shock. Suddenly, his innate focus returned with a vengeance. Mike realized he *could* do something to make a positive difference in his life and in the lives of others. He could use his theatre background to speak out about rape!

The idea that there was a real place he could put his energies shook him out of his self-pity and got him up off his BUT—but now he faced a whole slew of potential BUTS!

The year was 1990. Who was going to listen to a twenty-year-old college student talk about such a sensitive issue? Even schools were avoiding discussing rape. Mike had nowhere to go, yet he didn't sit down on his BUT. He did what he does best: he focused on what he knew he could do.

He sent a flier to the faculty at his own college, the University of Wisconsin at Whitewater, offering to speak to their classes about rape. Two faculty members contacted him, and he spoke—actually, it was more like a chat. Over time, Mike would develop these chats into an interactive and fun presentation.

Within two years, Mike had spoken to over forty schools in southeastern Wisconsin. At the same time, he became a peer educator on campus and served on a sexual assault task force for the entire campus (all while remaining active with the swim team and as head of a student organization in the business school).

During the next nine years, he helped support his wife and three sons by taking out loans to keep him speaking, doing high school coaching, working in the corporate world, and running an entertainment company. All this time, he continued to speak periodically.

After getting advice from two speaker colleagues, Mike decided to follow his passion. He sold his small entertainment business for almost no profit and devoted himself to his speaking career. At first, he was broke. Creditors were calling because the family was living off credit cards. Yet Mike and his wife, Karen, just kept reminding each other why they were on this mission. They wanted to stop sexual assaults from happening.

After a while, people began asking Mike, "Why don't you have a book?" Mike realized that he *did* have a book— inside his head. All he had to do was let it out. So for ten days, he typed and typed and typed. Out of those ten days came *May I Kiss You?*, a book on healthy dating, consent, and sexual assault awareness.

Almost overnight, he went from speaking periodically to being one of the most sought-after education speakers in North America. Mike went on to found an educational organization called the Date Safe Project. It didn't happen by magic, however. It happened because he refused to sit on his BUT.

All too often in my work, I meet people whose lives have been ravaged by sexual assault. It is a terrible thing, and very difficult to get past. These people are justifiably angry and distraught, as Mike was. Yet what inspires me most about Mike is that he had the same choice as every relative of a sexual assault survivor: to focus on the anger and unfairness of the rape or to focus on the opportunity to make a difference in a world that didn't really want to discuss the difficult topic of verbal sexual consent. The result of his choice to focus on the opportunity to make a difference is now helping hundreds of thousands of young adults date more safely, respect themselves, and speak out against sexual assault.

LESSON 5

Choose Your Friends Wisely

By the time he was twenty-one, Gary Coxe had been through a mind-boggling series of tragedies: his father was murdered, his wife told him his baby wasn't really his, and he'd built—and lost—a $100,000-a-year business. Now he is a wildly successful multimillionaire, a speaker and personal growth coach who owns private jets and helicopters. And I was a kid just out of college, looking for some pointers from a master. I couldn't even believe he had (finally!) agreed to talk with me on the phone. I never would have thought in a thousand years that this conversation would change the way I looked at my friends forever.

It all began with an innocent question. "Gary," I asked, "if you had the opportunity to share only one piece of advice with someone on how to succeed, what would you tell him?"

"Hmm . . . Only one piece? Okay, here it is: be careful who you complain to."

What the heck was he talking about? Complain to? How do complaining and success even come into the same equation? Fortunately, he clued me in.

"Sean," he explained, "a real friend is someone you call when you're having a bad day. Think about it. Do you call your obnoxious neighbor, your boss, or your enemy on a bad day? No, you call your friend."

I couldn't argue with that!

"So," he continued, "what type of response would a *real* friend have to your complaints?" He didn't wait for me to answer. "Here's my rule of thumb," he said. "A good-quality friend won't join in with you. They will either help you fix the issue or help you let go of the negativity you're tangled up in."

Whoa. I'd never really thought about it before, but he was so right. If you complain to a friend and she joins in with you, she stirs up your anger or sadness and actually makes your situation worse. I've seen so many people get off their BUTS and make huge strides in their health, wealth, and relationships—only to be shot down and torn apart by their "friends." Soon they begin to link progress and growth to the sensation of pain, and retreat to their BUTS. This is the kind of power our friends hold over us.

"Sean," said Gary, "the people we hang out with have a tremendous impact on our lives. Maybe more than you've considered."

After I got off the phone, Gary's words stayed with me. I began to notice more and more how profoundly the quality and course of our lives are influenced by the people we choose to call our friends.

How We Become Our Friends

Right about now, you may be thinking, "Sean, that's ridiculous! Maybe it's true for some people, but I don't cave to peer pressure. Sure, maybe when I was a kid . . . but I'm an adult now. I do what I want!"

I used to think the same thing . . . until I began doing some research and paying attention to my life and that of others. What I discovered shocked me. In fact, we become *exactly* like those we hang out with most. Think about it . . .

Just as a goldfish swimming in a tank of diseased water inevitably becomes sick, a human hanging out in a toxic peer group eventually becomes toxic. When you place yourself in an environment, you eventually become the environment. It's inevitable.

The right group of companions can be the greatest asset to your success and well-being. The wrong group, however, can tear your life to pieces and send you careening off a cliff. I can't overstress the importance of this understanding. The truth is, if you take action on all the other lessons in this book but overlook this one, everything you've achieved will eventually be undermined.

The Pit Crew Theory of Friendship

One evening, I was sprawled out on my hotel bed, flipping through the TV channels trying to find some mildly entertaining background noise as I prepared for a speech the next morning. I couldn't find anything, so I hit the mute button and went back to concentrating on my speech.

After about an hour or so, I looked back up at the TV. I was about to hit the power button to turn it off when the TV suddenly spoke to me. It said, "Sean, don't turn me off." Okay, fine, so maybe it didn't *literally* speak to me . . . yet the program that was on seemed to speak directly to a concept I was working on. I started paying attention.

The show was all about high-performance auto racing. I watched, mesmerized, as the cars zipped around and around the track at speeds nearing 200 mph. At some point, each car had to pull off the track. While the driver waited behind the wheel, a team of mechanics and technicians streamed around it—changing tires, checking fluid levels, and generally doing everything that needed to be done to get the car and driver back on the track at optimal effectiveness. Wait a minute . . . there was something there if I could only figure it out . . . *Eureka!*

I'd been searching for a metaphor to help me convey the idea I'd learned from Gary that the people with whom you surround yourself determine how far you go in life. I had already discarded some overused and not-quite-right analogies:

Birds of a feather flock together.

A chain is only as strong as its weakest link.

When you lay down with dogs you wake up with fleas.

Now, thanks to this hotel television, I had discovered an original metaphor that made the idea crystal clear: the pit crew!

These multimillion-dollar race cars had pretty impressive pit crews. But what if the pit crews didn't have the cars' best interests in mind? I began to imagine a different scenario . . .

- The mechanic designated to change the tires comes moseying out to the car empty-handed and tells the driver, sorry, but he's used the new tires for his own car. I call this *taker* behavior.
- Then the guy who's supposed to refuel the car walks over to the gas tank and pokes holes in it, causing every remaining drop of fuel to leak out. I call this *drainer* behavior.
- Finally, a person with a giant wrench begins smashing the heck out of the engine—laughing like crazy. I call this *destroyer* behavior.

With takers, drainers, and destroyers in the driver's pit crew, there's *no way* he or she would be able to win a race. Actually, the car wouldn't even be able to get back on the track.

Choosing Your Pit Crew

I see takers, drainers, and destroyers in human pit crews every day—they surround so many of the people who come to me wondering how their lives got so off course. It's a sad truth, but we humans often make horrible choices in the company we keep. High-performance race cars are expensive vehicles, but you and I are priceless. We deserve the best pit crews possible. Anything less, and we'll end up losing the "human race."

Avoid the Takers

The mechanic who took the race car tires and used them on his own car was a *taker*. I'll bet you know at least one person in your life who mooches off you, selfishly using your money, talents, social network, or belongings. Maybe you even tolerate it. Don't! These friends take far more from us than they ever contribute.

Recently, I recognized that one of my longtime friends was a taker. I'd known him for years, and I'd even looked up to him as a mentor. Because of this, I overlooked the warning signs. But one day, when our friendship was tested, his true nature revealed itself, and I couldn't help but see it.

I had met a girl online, and we'd talked on the phone, text-messaged, and e-mailed each other for a couple of months. I'd begun to develop some real interest in her, and she seemed to be reciprocating. We decided to meet in person, so I invited her to see me present a talk in the town where she lived. I also invited twelve of my other friends—some of the twenty-five or so friends that I call my "Seantourage"—including my old buddy.

Afterward, we all had dinner together. I looked across the table and was shocked to see my buddy hitting on the girl I was interested in. I quickly excused myself and asked him to join me for a minute. I explained the whole situation, getting him up to speed on who she was and how I felt she had great relationship potential for me. I told him clearly that I'd appreciate it if he didn't hit on her. He acknowledged my concern and agreed to respect my wishes. Three days later, I discovered that he had asked her for her number later that night and afterward pursued her romantically.

I felt that like a punch in the gut. I knew that even though we'd been friends for years—or at least I thought we had been—I had to cut him from my pit crew: not because he "won" the girl I liked, but because it was so easy for him to disregard not only my feelings but a direct request!

Takers like this man have no regard for you, your wishes, or your boundaries. Let them go before they take something even more precious from you.

Avoid the Drainers

Now let's talk about the member of the pit crew who pokes holes in your gas tank. These people are *drainers*—they drain your energy, bringing drama, darkness, and negativity into your life. Every time they show up, the energy in the room plummets. You feel as if you need a week at a spa just to recover from hanging out with them. My friend James Ray says it best: "Stay away from energy vampires!"

No matter how strong you are, drainers will eventually suck the life out of you and suck you into their depressing world. You can spot them easily by listening to what they talk about; negative statistics, scary news stories, health warnings, and horrifying, terrible personal accounts are par for the course:

"Did you hear about the rise in lung cancer in women?"

"You'd better be careful on the Internet—I heard about this guy who lost everything he owned just because he registered on a Web site."

"Man, the government is so crooked, they just take your money and spend it on themselves."

"Just yesterday, I saw a bunny get run over by a semi."

Not every conversation you have with your friends needs to be about upbeat topics, of course. You should be able to talk about all kinds of things. Yet if you begin to notice that certain friends can talk only about what's wrong,

bad, and unfair with the world and their life—and, by exten-
sion, your life—that's a sign that you're talking to a drainer.

You have only so much energy, right? If you let these
energy vampires drain you dry, you'll have nothing left for
yourself.

Avoid the Destroyers

Back to our auto racing metaphor. The mechanic who
trashed the engine with a wrench was a *destroyer*. Destroyers
in your pit crew are the worst. They actually get a thrill out
of destroying minds, bodies, spirits, dreams, opportunities,
and property. Sometimes they do this unconsciously, without even realizing it, but sometimes they do it on purpose.
These are the so-called friends who pressure us to drink to
get drunk, to always blow off our work and play, to quit on
our dreams, to break the law, to do something unethical or
immoral . . . the list goes on and on.

Destroyers are angry people. They show the world
they don't care by challenging authority and laying waste
to everything they come into contact with. They'll lie to
your face and think nothing of it. They'll ruin a surprise
party you've been planning for months. They'll share your
secrets in a public gathering just to embarrass you. They'll
overpromise to get immediate praise and then underdeliver
when it matters most.

I once had a destroyer in my life who was a lot of fun
to be around—at least when we were partying. He was high
energy and very loud. At a crazy college party, that's a plus.

At your grandparents' house for dinner . . . not so good. Every time I was around him, I'd make sure we were somewhere very loud or very obscure. Why? Because I didn't want him around my family or someone who might be important to my career or anyone who might be sensitive to the inappropriate comments that would inevitably fly out of his mouth. He was a social liability, to say the least.

Destroyers feel they have nothing to live for outside of seeing what they can get away with. The fact that their actions have negative consequences for others rarely—if ever—registers on their radar. Their behavior often leads them to bankruptcy, alcoholism, divorce, obesity, prison, homelessness, drug addiction, depression, and complete and total abandonment of everyone around them.

They can lead you to the same place if you don't take action to cut them from your pit crew.

GET OFF YOUR BUT *NOW!*
Who's on Your Pit Crew?

Take a good, honest look at the people you have selected to be in your pit crew. Have you drafted any takers, drainers, or destroyers? In your Get Off Your BUT Now! journal, make a list of your top five friends, the people you call when you're having a bad day. Ask yourself if they are taking from, draining, or destroying you in any way.

This activity may be difficult because it forces you to look at the company you're keeping. Remember: the quality of your life is hanging in the balance. If you keep negative pit crew members on your team, your dreams and your feeling of well-being are paying the price.

Why We Keep Takers, Drainers, and Destroyers Around

If they're so awful, why do we keep takers, drainers, and destroyers in our lives? The reasons vary:

- We feel sorry for them.
- We feel obligated to them.
- We think we can change them.
- We're afraid of what would happen if we left them.
- We're addicted to the drama they provide.
- We like having someone to make fun of.
- We have a history with them stretching back to childhood.
- We want something from them.
- We feel better about our lives when we see them.

Mostly, however, we haven't truly recognized or admitted to ourselves the sizable damage they've done to our lives.

As annoying and destructive as they are, takers, energy drainers, and destroyers are generally not evil people—they are people who need help. But unless they come to you specifically asking for that help, you need to stay out of it. You're welcome to throw them a life vest, but I'm warning you: if you get in the water and try to pull them ashore, they'll wrap their dead weight around you and drag you to the bottom of the ocean floor.

GET OFF YOUR BUT *NOW!*
What Kind of Pit Crew Member Are You?

At this point, when you're eyeing all your old friends and sizing them up to see if they belong in your pit crew, it's important to remember a painful reality: *we are responsible for our behavior in the lives of our friends.* Are we taking from, draining, or destroying the lives of our friends without even realizing it?

Remember: you not only have a pit crew around you but also are an important member of your friends' crews.

This exercise is very straightforward, but it asks you to be ready to accept the truth: call up your five closest friends and ask them to be really candid in their response to what you will be saying. Explain that you want to be a better friend, and fill them in briefly on the basics of what you've learned in this chapter. Then ask them if they feel that you've taken from, drained, or destroyed them in any way. If you have, apologize, tell them that you value their friendship, and ask how you can better serve them as a friend.

The ABC's of Friendship

Relax. I'm not suggesting that you need to scrap your entire pit crew and recruit a new batch of friends. You just need to consider how much time you want to spend with certain people. The more time you spend with someone, the more you become like that person.

Wait—doesn't that mean that a positive person could boost up a negative person? No, it doesn't. In order to move from a negative space to a positive one, you have to be willing to change. But negativity doesn't need your consent to affect you.

This is why I split my pit crew into three groups:

1. **A Friends**—friends I **A**lways want to be around
2. **B Friends**—friends I want to **B** careful of
3. **C Friends**—friends I want to say "**C** ya later!" to

This ranking system has nothing to do with how much I like or love an individual. It simply describes the amount of time I can afford to spend in that person's company.

A Friends are genuine friends. When you're having a bad day, they pick you up, dust you off, and give you a loving shove in the direction of your dreams. They join you in making healthy choices—being honest with yourself, digging deeper to find out what you're really complaining about, eating right, exercising, going on spiritual explorations, engaging in creative activities. You know they'll drop everything if you're in a jam. When they commit to something, they always follow through. They consider your feelings before saying or doing anything. A Friends are the hardest to find, and they are truly priceless.

C Friends (don't worry, we'll come back to the B Friends in a moment!) are the extreme takers, energy drainers, and destroyers. Don't walk away from them . . . run! Any time you hang out with a C Friend, your quality of life will slip. Constant exposure to them will quickly lead to you being sick, tired, and broke. Not a good idea.

The majority of your friends will probably fall into the B category. Sometimes they seem positive and supportive, like A Friends, and at other times they're negative and destructive, like C Friends. You never know who will show up when you hang out with them. They'll say nice things to your face and say mean things behind your back. They'll tell you they'll always be there for you, but when it's inconvenient, they're gone.

Our B Friends tend to sort themselves out after a while. Either they eventually grow up, get serious, and make positive strides to be an A Friend, or they never get it (or never care to) and eventually get bumped to the C Friend list and out the door.

Welcoming A Friends into Your Life

Your goal from this day forward is to recruit A Friends into your pit crew. In a world overpopulated by B and C Friend behaviors, doing this may take some time.

Have no fear! It takes only a few A Friends—or even one—to transform your life. You just need to know the signs to look for when manifesting these high-caliber individuals in your life. You also need to know where to look.

The quickest way to figure out if a person is A Friend material is by meeting and observing his closest friends. Remember, we become like our friends. So right away, by spending time with him and his close friends, you can see what he's like. If you spot takers, drainers, or destroyers in the crowd, there's a high likelihood that your A Friend candidate is in one of those three categories as well. Proceed with great caution.

Another clue is to watch how the individual reacts under pressure. Does she flip out and make really big deals about little things? Red flag! Is she loving and supportive to people, without regard to personal gain? Green light!

It's especially important to see how they treat children. They may not have any kids themselves, or even want kids, and that's fine. The key is to see how they respond in the presence of children. If they're uncomfortable and irritable, that's a good sign that they lack patience and compassion.

A Friends are not necessarily the life of the party, and they may or may not have a lot of friends themselves. Never assume that because a person has too many or too few friends (in your opinion), he is (or is not) a potential A Friend.

Where to Find A Friends
You wouldn't go to a heavy metal concert and expect to meet opera aficionados, right? So if you're looking for

A Friends, ask yourself where you would be most likely to find them. Personally, I've never made an A Friend at a bar. Bars, although they can be fun, are usually filled with people who are seeking noisy distraction or instant gratification, or a way to drown their sorrows or numb their insecurities.

My potential A Friends tend to turn up at personal growth seminars, places of worship and meditation, healthy restaurants, adventure clubs, bookstores, coffee shops, gyms, and dinner parties given by other A Friends. Two themes characterize all these venues: *upbeat* and *health conscious*. A Friends treat their mind, body, and spirit with love and respect. Naturally they are inclined to love, respect, and care for others with the same devotion.

A Friends in Action

You might feel that I'm taking this A, B, and C Friend stuff too seriously. I'm not. Most people don't take this seriously enough. Not having A Friends you can count on is guaranteed to lead you into a life of upset. You'll be stuck on the side of the road with a flat tire, calling around for help, and your B and C Friends will be nowhere to be found. You'll be curled up on the bathroom floor sick as a dog, and your B and C Friends will be mysteriously busy. You'll be sitting at a diner all alone, crying your eyes out because a relationship just ended, and your B and C Friends . . . well, you get the picture.

Several years ago, I came through an unexpected emotional crisis in one piece, thanks to two of my A Friends.

I had just completed a very intense psychology training in dealing with heavy emotional challenges. The instructor warned the class to go home and just take it easy for the evening. He cautioned us not to go out socializing, as our own issues might surface because of the process we'd just gone through.

I was the youngest student in the course and thought I knew it all. Of course, I didn't. I figured I could handle it— no problem. Anyway, it was my last night in town. I was entitled to some fun! So instead of having a quiet night to myself, I went to a big party with my buddies John and Jeremy.

For the first fifteen minutes, everything was fine. Then I found myself focusing in on what I had been trained to see: everyone's nonverbal insecurities. This brought all of my own insecurities—which had been stirred up all day— to the surface. I couldn't stop obsessing. I began fearing that I would never be able to socialize in public again because all I would ever be able to see is people's pain. I was completely terrified. My heart was pounding like crazy and felt as if it were going to explode.

John and Jeremy noticed right away that I wasn't looking very good. Even though we had driven a long distance to get to the party and it was filled wall to wall with beautiful girls and tons of great food, they just turned my wheelchair around and headed back to the car with me. Never once did they whine or complain about leaving. Their concern for my health and wellness trumped all of their pleasure-seeking desires.

As John fastened me into the child's car seat that I ride in, he asked, "You all right, Seanny?"

"No, I'm not," I said. "Can we just sit in the car for a while?"

So my friends and I just sat there, and that was good—because the next minute I lost it completely. Tears poured down my face, and I started sobbing loudly. My nose was running profusely, and I began to shake uncontrollably. Later, they told me this went on for fifteen minutes straight. Every personal issue that I was battling in my life at the time came bubbling up, right there in the back seat of my buddy's car. I had been trying so hard to create the persona of someone who had it all together. I had tried to act as if nothing were too big for me to handle and that nothing could rattle me in life. The pressure of keeping this façade going had finally become too much. I'd hit a breaking point. I couldn't have contained those emotions if I'd tried.

Finally, my tears subsided. John and Jeremy were look-ing at me as though they had just witnessed an exorcism. Once they realized I had come out the other side, however, they calmly smiled and welcomed me back.

"You feel better now?" asked John.

"Is there anything we can do for you?" asked Jeremy.

"You already have." I felt completely at peace.

Just by being intuitive enough to leave the party with me, stay in the car, and not say a word, they had helped me tremendously. Never once did they tease me about the expe-rience, and all these years later, they never have. I asked them then not to share the experience with anyone, and to the best of my knowledge they kept that pledge.

This is A Friend behavior. B Friends would probably not have left the party; C Friends would not have cared (or even noticed) how I felt, and they probably would have tormented me for experiencing such an extremely emotional moment. Sadly, we live in a society where men are discouraged from showing pain and sadness. Crying in front of your buddies is judged by many guys as a sign of weakness, but not by my handpicked group of A Friends. My buddies make no apologies for being human and having emotions.

To finish out the night on a higher note, we drove out to the beach and just sat in the car, talking and laughing for hours. I couldn't help but think of the famous line that Clarence the angel inscribed in the book he gave to George Bailey at the end of the movie It's a Wonderful Life: "Remember, George, no man is a failure who has friends."

If I were inscribing this book to you, I'd amend that line just a bit:

"No one is a failure who has *A Friends!*"

Letting Go of B's and C's

By now you're probably wondering, "Sean, does this mean I have to dump my B and C Friends right away?"

Of course not! I'm certainly not suggesting that you whip out your cell phone and call all your friends and let them know what category they're in. It won't go over well if you call up a friend and say, "Listen, I just read this book.

Apparently, you're a B Friend—I'm watching you. Turn into an A Friend or else!"

No, that's not a good idea. The main point is to learn to pay attention to the people you surround yourself with and how they make you feel. Once you do that, the sorting process will take care of itself.

Sometimes, though, it does become necessary to let someone know you no longer want to have a relationship with him or her. Whenever I present this idea to clients or groups, someone always asks, "Isn't that cruel? Don't they deserve another chance?"

Letting go of friends should *never* be a cruel process. And yes, almost everyone deserves a second chance. In some cases, third and fourth chances might be a good idea. But when you find yourself giving someone his twenty-fifth chance, the likelihood that he is going to change any time soon is very small. If a person continues to take from you, drain your energy, or destroy your life, and you continue to allow it, you are just as responsible for the pain as she is. A buddy of mine once told me that he had a roommate who kept stealing from him. When my friend confronted him, the roommate said, "Well, you kept giving me the opportunity, so I kept taking it."

Here's how to let go kindly, but firmly:

Sit the person down privately and make it very clear that you do not appreciate her behavior. Let her know that you deserve better. Tell her that if she wants to continue to be in your life, you need her to respect your requests and your boundaries. If she doesn't come around, then make it clear you have to go your separate ways. Tell her you love her, but now you're forced to love her from a distance.

Then say good-bye, and don't look back.

GET OFF YOUR BUT *NOW!*
What Do You Look For?

Take out your Get Off Your BUT Now! journal and write your responses to these questions. Try to list five qualities for each.

What qualities did you set as "must-haves" when you chose your current friends?

What are some qualities you've overlooked that need to be added?

What are some qualities you need to embody if you want to attract more amazing pit crew members into your life?

It can be easy to overlook your friends' less desirable qualities because you think there's no problem as long as you're having fun with them. The ability to have fun is an important quality, but it's not enough to qualify a person as an A Friend!

Being an A Friend

When life breaks you down, you want to be able to screech into your pit and have fresh tires prepped and ready, a full tank of gas just waiting to be pumped, and the best engine technician on hand to rush to your aid. That requires A Friends on your pit crew—and the best way to ensure this is to be an A Friend yourself.

Here's what I promise to bring into the lives of my A Friends: a hunger for knowledge, a willingness to run in the rain, an endless pursuit in making the world a better place, a trust in my intuition, no fear of being purely honest, commitment to being fiercely loyal, a charming glow, an infectious amount of enthusiasm, a never-ending resiliency in the face of adversity, a tolerance for those who live a life different from my own, and a wise ability to discern the times to praise, critique, console, and surrender.

You Do Not Have to Be Lonely

Recently, I asked a very wealthy client of mine about his friendships. He looked at me oddly. "Sean," he said, "it's been over a decade since I've hung out with or even received a call from a friend. I have no friends."

Personally, I can't imagine such a lonely existence, and I used to feel tons of pity for people who live life without friends. Now, however, I realize that it's no accident. This man, for example, had been bitter about his life. He had never wanted to make any sacrifices for anyone else. Clearly, he had closed off any doors a potential friend might walk through. He had also been hurt early in life and had put up a wall around himself so that no one could even begin to get close. He let no one in.

I made it clear to him in the session that he needed to forgive those he felt wronged by. As long as he held animosity toward them, he would push away any chance of letting new people in. I explained that all anger directed toward others was taking from, draining, and destroying his own life.

I spent a considerable amount of time showing him that what took place with everyone he felt hurt by originated because he chose to associate with people who weren't of the highest caliber. By upgrading his peer group to A Friends, those experiences wouldn't be repeated. By the end of our session, he realized that friendship is all about opening up and letting in the highest-quality people you can find. It's about trusting a person enough to know that your dreams are supported and safe in his airspace, as well as supporting him in the same way when he needs it.

Slowly, my formerly friendless client began to open himself to people. Making each new friend became a revelation of support and love that helped wash away the pain and hurt he had lived with for so many years.

In our next and final lesson, I will guide you through a process that will release the pain from your past relationships (both platonic and romantic) so that you can clearly decipher who would be best to draft into your pit crew. Yet even with the strongest pit crew, you still have to face the biggest hurdle alone: taking responsibility for your past, present, and future. Owning the good, the bad, and the ugly truth of where you are and where you're headed will become your secret weapon. In the final lesson, I will show you how to forge and brandish such a weapon so that nothing can stop you from seizing your dreams.

HOW PETER GOT OFF HIS BUT

"I would stay in school, BUT I'm in too much credit card debt."

I'm constantly refining my pit crew: adding new people to the mix, sending some to the bench, and cutting a few from the team entirely. I am blessed to say that I have dozens of friends. Yet only a few are as close to me as my A+ Friend Peter Bielagus. He's one of the most confident, level-headed guys I know. So when he told me his story one night over dinner, I was shocked. I couldn't believe Peter would ever have fallen prey to the trap he landed in when he was just starting college. Seeking the approval and acceptance of his college peer group almost cost him his education.

In the late 1990s, Peter was blasted with credit card offers both in person and through the mail. What college student isn't? On his college campus, credit card companies were even allowed to set up tables in the student union and in high-traffic hallways.

Sometimes the tables were managed by attractive sorority girls, sometimes even flat-out models. You've probably seen these tables yourself—in shopping malls, fairgrounds, sporting events, and concerts. They'll give you a mountain of gifts for free—movie tickets, pizza coupons, mugs, T-shirts, stuffed animals, pens that light up, Frisbees . . . if you just fill out an application.

Like a lot of students, Peter thought, *Hey, what's the risk?* Even if you were turned down for the card, you could still keep your free gift! At every chance he got, Peter would fill out a form, carefully choose his free gift from the display table, and briskly walk away, laughing inside and thinking (as most do), "Suckers!"

Except . . . it turned out that my buddy Peter was the real sucker, just as credit card companies knew he would be. One night, his friends were all going out, and he was out of cash. He charged the evening's entertainment on his credit card. Like most folks, Peter wasn't worried about a few small charges here or there.

One of those "small" charges would be for a $300 night of clubbing in South Beach, with Peter playing the role of a South Florida Santa Claus. These "here or there" occurrences became commonplace. Soon, my buddy Pete began to notice how many friends he had when he was the one buying. It felt good!

So when the credit card bills arrived every month, he always made just the minimum payment and kept partying. Then, in February of his freshman year, he received a bill for his Chase Manhattan credit card—and he didn't have enough money for the minimum payment. At the time, Peter was just a kid—he knew nothing about credit cards, their high interest rates, or their steep late fees. But he was smart enough to know that if he owed $5,000 and the company was only asking for a $110 minimum payment and he couldn't even make that ... well, something must be terribly wrong.

Peter was not a rich college kid. In fact, he was on financial aid. He had a job that paid just above minimum wage, and the other temp jobs he was scrambling for paid just about as much. And he already was a full-time student, so he could only work so many hours. When he paid that Chase credit card bill late, the company didn't get mad at him—it just charged him a late fee and raised his rate.

Peter was caught in a vicious circle. He really wanted to get out of debt, yet the whole reason he got into debt was because he was broke. And he was still broke. If anything, he was more broke. "I'd like to pay this off," he thought, "BUT it's not like I can get a third job." There was nothing he could do. Had he sat there on his BUT, continuing to get pummeled with high interest and slapped with the occasional late fee because he was waiting for a paycheck, he would be buried in debt today.

Peter, however, refused to sit on his BUT.

It didn't take reading more than a few personal finance books for Peter to realize how much this credit card debt was going to hurt his financial life. He worried that he would have to drop out of school just to pay off his debt. He stopped spending right away. Sadly, once his credit card vanished from the club scene, his so-called friends disappeared before last call. Back then, of course, he'd never heard me talk about A, B, and C Friends—yet he quickly realized that these people hadn't been friends at all. His pit crew was decimated, and he was desolated.

One night, discouraged and frustrated, he found himself sitting at a bar, all alone. He'd stopped spending, but he was about to fall back on another BUT: "BUT I don't have any friends! I may as well just get drunk." He ordered a drink, thinking that maybe he could drown his sorrows away. As he lifted the glass to his mouth he suddenly thought, This is ridiculous! I'm just a college student. My life is not over! He put the beer down untouched, and walked out of the bar.

The first thing he did was banish the BUTS and replace them with YETS. "I don't have any more free time to get an extra job," he realized, "yet I can bike to school and save money on gas. I can't ask my boss for a raise, yet I can start packing my own lunch instead of buying fast food every day." These and other small changes allowed him to add an extra $5 or $10 to his credit card payments each month. Many people don't realize this, but even such small amounts can often cut your credit card payoff time in half. Soon these extra $5 payments became extra $50 payments. In four short years (still earning a lousy wage and being a full-time student), that credit card debt was gone.

Today, more than ten years later, Peter is a licensed financial adviser who travels the world speaking to students and service members about getting out of debt and jump-starting their financial lives. He's published two books, has a Web site, bought a house with an ocean view, and travels the world for pleasure whenever he wants. And none of that would have ever happened if he'd let the size of his financial BUT hold him down.

As I said, Peter's story shocked me. Why? It wasn't as terrible and heart-wrenching as so many I'd heard—he was eighteen and in debt; that was all. Yet I couldn't help thinking about what might have happened to Peter if he *hadn't* gotten off his BUTS: I have no doubt that his C Friends would have kept him spending, his drinking would have interfered with his schoolwork, his debts would have kept piling up . . . and instead of being one of my very best friends, he would still be mired in debt, looking around at his life and wondering what the heck happened.

If you feel trapped by debt or some other life circumstance, your first and biggest challenge will be to get off the BUT that got you there in the first place. Although it won't be easy, if you follow in Peter's steps, it will be possible.

LESSON 6

Take Full Responsibility

It's amazing what kinds of thoughts race through your mind at 3:00 AM when you're lying in a hospital emergency room in terrible pain. I was afraid that every breath I took could be my last. You can't buy that kind of oxygen.

Why couldn't this have happened when I was home, near a hospital I was familiar with? Life doesn't work that way, though. It doesn't conveniently schedule your illnesses and accidents—or even your own death. These things barge in like a drunk uncle, unannounced and unwelcomed.

I couldn't believe it was happening—not this way, not now. I didn't know if I should be crying, screaming, or pleading. What is the protocol for terror?

My body felt as if a football-size bomb had lodged in my lower back and burst in my abdomen. In a matter of minutes, the pressure became so intense that I could no longer sit up. My body grew terribly cold, and I began to shake uncontrollably. I didn't care who saw me shaking.

All the ego-driven qualities like wanting to look cool and
be seen as powerful drained out of me.

I was going to die. I knew it.

Near Death

One year earlier, when my best friend, John, announced
that he was getting married to his girlfriend, Amy, he told
me that they wanted me in their wedding. I was flattered.

"I've never been asked to be a groomsman before,"
I told him.

"No, Sean, that's not what we're asking. We want you
to perform the wedding ceremony."

"Wow! I'm so honored."

So I went online and got the proper certification, and
in October 2007, I flew to San Francisco to unite two souls
for eternity. At least that's what I thought I was going to do.

I attended the wedding rehearsal and dinner and then
retired for the evening. As John wheeled me back to my
room, I told him that something didn't feel right in my body.
I chalked it up to gas pains and went to bed. I never went
to sleep. At around 2:30 AM, the pain got so intense I knew
I had to go to the hospital. Something was really wrong. I was
terrified.

Thank God I was not alone. Far from it. My parents, my
cousins, and John's dad were right by my side in the emergency room. My mind reacted to the terror by switching over

to sensory recorder mode, taking in all the minute-by-minute details we normally overlook: the faint smell of hand sanitizer, the brightly colored scrubs worn by the nurses working the graveyard shift, the steady hum of the air filtration system.

Meanwhile, my pain was growing worse by the second. I began comparing the intensity to past pains I had experienced: Is this worse than a broken collarbone? It climbed the charts in quite a hurry, quickly surpassing the pain of broken ribs and broken arms, and rapidly approaching the pain of a metal rod being pulled from my leg . . . Could it really get that bad? Oh, God, I hoped not.

A nurse was trying to get my attention. "Mr. Stephenson, I need to ask you a few important questions. This will only take a minute." She began rattling off a series of "are you allergic to" questions. No. No. No. Then she landed on a question I wasn't expecting.

"Sir, do you practice any religious denomination?"

What? I just wanted to be drugged and fixed by a seasoned doctor who had dedicated his entire life's purpose to alleviating the kind of pain I was in and would assure me I was going to make it. How is that relevant to what my spiritual practice is? But I was way beyond engaging her in conversation. I just barked out "Catholic!" and tried not to scream.

As she scratched her pen across her notes, she stopped and looked at me. "Would you like me to contact a priest, sir?"

Click!

The recorder shut off.

Inside the Theater of My Mind

My head nodded yes to her question, but I was no longer in that room. The Sean that is writing to you right now was gone. I had left the building.

My senses dulled to a level barely operable, and I went deep inside. The world outside, from which I had felt so separated many times in my life, was gone. All I could hear was my internal voice, all I could see were the images in my mind, and all I could feel (besides the pain) were the tears that streamed down my face.

Then gravity seemed to go into reverse. Everything was flipped upside down, and I was no longer lying on the earth; the earth was now right on top of my chest, pushing me down. One by one, the portals to the outside world began to close. My mind was shutting itself in—boarding up the windows and closing down my senses against the whirlwind it must have sensed was coming. Then everything went numb. Was I dying, or just powering down to a level where my body could reserve all its energy for healing? I didn't know, and I was in too much pain to care.

The world became dark, silent, and still.

Then, from behind me, a light came on. I was in . . . a movie theater?

Of course. Movies had been my guilty pleasure my entire life. I'd seen almost every box office hit since I was a little boy. I spent more money on theater tickets and video rentals than anyone I had ever met. I'd always felt safe in movie theaters. I guess my unconscious mind knew that if it put me there now, I would pay close attention to whatever was projected on the screen. And I did.

The images on the screen started flashing one by one, like a slow-moving slide show. I saw pictures of everyone I had ever loved in my life, beginning with the nurses who had dubbed me King Tut in the delivery room on the day I entered into this world all mangled and in a heap of excruciating pain.

I began praying, right there in the theater of my mind, that I wouldn't have to leave the world in as much discomfort as I had entered it with. If that was my destiny, I sure didn't feel ready. Then the slide show began to go faster.

Mom, Dad, Heidi, and my whole extended family appeared, followed by my kindergarten teacher, the ice cream man who drove up and down my street in the summer when I was a kid, my childhood friends . . . Doug, Dave, Tucker, Joanne, Katy . . . they were all there, in their innocence.

The girl down the street who leaned over my wheelchair and pressed her lips against mine, delivering my first kiss.

All the heroic school teachers who came to my house and got down on the floor next to me to teach me math, science, history, and English as I was wrapped in bandages and reeling with pain.

My first girlfriend in junior high, who broke up with me in a note she left in my locker. Now, as I watched her picture projected on the screen, I felt no anger toward her. We were so young. She was just a casualty of a lousy pit crew that didn't support her affinity for a little boy in a wheelchair who made her feel so warm inside.

With each passing slide on the screen, my heart felt unconditional love and complete forgiveness for all those who I felt had ever "wronged me." If this was it for me, I would not leave this world with anger in my heart.

Now the images were flying by so fast that it felt as if I were viewing the entire collection of the *Sean Stephenson Times* on microfiche. Faster and faster it went. Boston Bill, Jeanine, Dr. Young, Tony Robbins, President Clinton . . . *oh, God, please slow down! I'm not ready for my life to end!* Now I was seeing images of my adult life. College professors, therapy clients, speaker colleagues . . . and they just kept coming. The pictures were so bright they were burning ghost images into the back of my mind.

And then the screen in front of me curled up along the edges, lifted off the wall, and wrapped around me a full 360 degrees. No matter where I looked, there I was. The images were swirling around, leaving me in the eye of a memory cyclone.

Then all my buddies, brothers from other mothers appeared. Followed by every girl I had ever loved as a friend or dated, kissed, or cuddled was now surrounding me. Off in the distance even my little reluctant rain runner was there.

Then a sea of unfamiliar people showed up. There were thousands of them. Who were they? Why were they appearing in this sacred moment? With a shock, I realized they were the thousands of people in my audiences over the entire span of my career as a speaker and media personality. I could feel their love for me too.

I felt so loved, yet so deeply sad. *I'm not ready to go!*

Then the screen went blank. The only sound was the unmistakable flapping of a filmstrip that had reached the end of its play and was whipping against the projector. And then even that sound faded off.

The movie of my life must be over. I began to get up from my seat and head for the exit, when the projector came back on. It was showing a horror flick. I sat down again.

There were no monsters, serials killers, or villainous aliens in this horror movie, but it was the scariest thing I had ever seen. It was a movie of everything I wanted to do in my life but had never gotten around to. I watched scene after scene of all the projects and ideas I'd had BUT had never had time for or energy for, or was afraid to commit to, or worried would result in failure . . . Now I was afraid none of them would ever materialize. *No! Let me out of here!*

"I WANT ANOTHER CHANCE!" I screamed to the invisible projectionist. "Please, I swear, I'll take responsibility for all my screwups and make more out of my life. I'm willing to endure whatever pain awaits me back in that emergency room and every day forward . . . I'm not ready to die!"

And then I collapsed to the floor of the theater, clutching my side. I felt as if someone were inside me, kicking me with steel cleats. It felt as if the outside world were coming back online. The dark theater vanished, replaced by fluorescent hospital lights that hurt my eyes. I heard the doctor say, "Sean, we need to move you to radiology for an MRI."

The movie of my life was over. It had taken only a moment. I was still here.

I'm Back

As I watched the white ceiling tiles whip by overhead, I realized I must be lying on a hospital gurney. My parents walked alongside, looking at me with concern, as the doctors explained that I had a kidney stone stuck in the tiny tube that traveled from the kidney to the bladder. The pain that consumed my every breath was the back pressure from the blocked kidney.

"During the next twenty-four hours, you may experience the most grueling pain of your life," one doctor said.

He was wrong! It turned out to be thirty-six hours. When the stone finally passed and the pain was miraculously gone, one thought filled me from head to toe:

I'm alive! I felt like Ebenezer Scrooge on Christmas morning. Like George Bailey at the end of It's a Wonderful Life, I wanted to race up the streets screaming at the top of my lungs, "Merry Christmas, Bedford Falls!" Never mind that it was October in San Francisco. I was beyond happy—I was elated. I still had time on the clock!

I could create the TV shows I'd always wanted to produce and star in, travel the world, go on a date with

Natalie Portman . . . I could write this book. Right after I was released from the hospital, I scribbled down a list of neglected goals on a napkin. It turned out to be one life-changing napkin that I've kept to this day.

I had returned to my normal life, but it looked anything but normal now. I saw all my unfinished business arrayed in front of me, with a bright spotlight shining on it, just waiting for me to *do something*. I had been forced to watch the movie of my life unfold as I lay near what I thought was death, but I needed to *own* my waking reality. I needed to take responsibility for my dreams and live out my full potential, a new movie: *Sean Stephenson's Second Chance.*

Was I really stuck in some celestial movie theater, given a chance to review my entire life by some divine power? Or was it all just a morphine-induced hallucination? All I can say is, it sure seemed real to me. And it was enough of a wake-up call for me to get off my BUT and spend several months of my life writing this book for you.

GET OFF YOUR BUT *NOW!*
Second Chance!

First, I want you to believe, just for this exercise, that today is your last day on earth.

Now, in your Get Off Your BUT *Now!* journal, name the ten people you really love in your life, the ones you are going to miss the most when you leave this earth. (If you don't have ten, that's okay.)

Next, list five to ten projects you've been dragging your feet on or have put on hold completely, and which you feel sad about never finishing.

Finally, list ten places you'll be sad that you never got to visit, or ten things you'll never get to do because today is your last day on earth.

Now:

Go tell those people you love them.

Go do the things you have been putting off.

Go visit those places and do those things you've always wanted to do.

Doing even one thing on your list will be the greatest gift you could give to yourself.

Owning Your Life

This last lesson is all about ownership—one of my favorite words in the English language. Until you own something, it owns you. It doesn't matter if it's an addiction, a fear, an excuse, or a thought. If you try to pass it off, deny it, or argue with its existence, it will continue to control your every move in life.

Hard-core? You'd better believe it!

The weakest people on the planet own nothing. I'm not talking about owning physical possessions; I'm talking about truly *meaningful* things: where they are in life, their physical health, the pain they've caused others, the good they've done others, their reaction to the abuse they've endured, the ways they've chosen to numb their pain, the direction in which their life is pointed. Until you own your life—the good and the bad—you're like a beached fish flopping around on land: you can move all you want, but you're not going anywhere.

The Freedom Formula

One of my wisest and most educated mentors is Dr. Matthew James, president of American Pacific University. He taught me a formula that helped me take ownership of my life and that is responsible for ending self-sabotage and allowing me to develop into the man I am today.

This formula is so simple, you might gloss right over it. Yet the best solutions are almost always simple—it's our problems that are complex. I've noticed that most of my clients have been mired in their complicated mind mess for so long, they feel that only a complicated solution will do the job. When I offer them this simple formula, their first response is often to thumb their nose at it in disgust.

You may be tempted to stand in disbelief, but stay with me. We'll get to it in a moment, I promise.

This formula has been so pivotal in my life that if I ever considered getting a tattoo—which I'm *not*, Mom, so relax—I would have this formula written on my hand so that it would be reinforced in my mind every day. In fact, one of my clients did just that after going through my Breakthrough Process (an intense, twelve-hour, full-emersion therapy session).

The more I test out this formula, the more it proves itself right, continually strengthening my commitment to it. I know that if you apply this formula to your life, you will see positive changes. Remarkable changes. In fact, once I get a client to accept the validity of this formula, 90 percent of our work is done. Unfortunately, if a client will not agree to work with this formula, I am forced to end the session and refund his money. Why? Because without acknowledgment of and commitment to this formula, all other therapeutic techniques will fail.

This is the formula:

C > E

See? I told you it was simple.

C stands for **Cause,** and **E** stands for **Effect. Cause is greater than Effect.** Each of us is living on one side or the other of this formula.

No matter which side we live on, we always get effects. The question is: Are these the effects we want?

When you live at the Cause end of the formula, *you* are the conscious mover of your life. When you are living at the Effect end of the formula, things just seem to "happen" to you. You are not in charge of your own life. Let's take a closer look at what it means to live at Cause and what it takes to live at Effect.

Living at Cause

We can tell that we're living at Cause when we have the results we really want out of life. For one person, this may mean making $100,000 a year, whereas another individual may want $100,000 a month. One person may want to train her body to enter an Iron Man Triathlon; another may just want to be in good enough shape to look decent in a swimsuit. One person may want to stay single and just date casually; another may want to be married and have children.

This equation doesn't judge *what* we want; it simply measures where we are in life. Do you have what you want? If you do, then you're already living at Cause. If you don't have what you really want, though, you'll need to change your way of thinking and acting. And that means taking responsibility for what happens to you.

When you live at Cause, you take full *responsibility* for everything that you have attracted into your life—the good and the bad. For most people, that is a very tough pill to swallow. We've all attracted negative scenarios, people, and events into our lives. Living at Cause doesn't mean feeling guilty or ashamed of what you have attracted to yourself. It means understanding that you are responsible for your actions—it is about *owning* your life and how it has transpired every step of the way.

Living at Effect

You are living at Effect if you have a pile of "reasons" for why you don't have what you want in life. Oh, how we love our reasons. Reasons are just excuses in fancy packaging. A reason is a two-syllable word for BUT—something we feel justified to sit back on in life.

We're living at Effect every time we blame someone or something else for our condition or status in life. The more we blame, the weaker we get, and the further we travel away from what we want most in life.

Effect is where most people live. In fact, most of this planet is living at Effect. The evidence is everywhere to be seen: divorce, disease, bankruptcy, depression, alcoholism, obesity, and the loss of the desire to live. It cripples people emotionally, mentally, and spiritually—much more profoundly than my brittle bones disorder.

Some days the stranglehold that Effect has on our society makes me want to cry, and other days it makes me want to scream. I'm often tempted to take out an ad in all the newspapers saying, "You are at the source of being fat, sick, tired, broke, angry, depressed, and lonely. Stop blaming your boss, family, neighbor, lover, government, society, or God. You are the one at the scene of the crime every time something goes wrong in your life. Stop looking for a fall guy, a scapegoat, or an innocent bystander to pin your problems on. Until you take ownership for your life, you will *always* be chasing happiness."

What—too direct?

I know. And it wouldn't work anyway. Remember, believing is seeing. As long as someone believes that her mother made her life miserable, that's all she'll ever be able to see.

Taking Out the Trash

I once explained the Freedom Formula to a client of mine, a woman who had been severely abused. She burst out in tears and said, "Are you saying I'm at fault for my father beating me as a child?"

"Of course not," I replied. "This isn't a matter of being at fault for being abused. This is a matter of being responsible for how you act in response to those events now. When you were little, you were right to do everything you needed to do to protect yourself. The question is, are you still curling up in a ball to fend off the blows of life, or are you standing tall?"

She just stared at me, puzzled. It was time to help her understand the difference between living at Cause and living at Effect.

"Grab your coat," I said, "we're going on a field trip." We left my office building and walked to a grassy field nearby. It was pouring rain and very windy, and the grass was littered with all kinds of trash that had blown in.

I handed her a plastic bag and rubber gloves and said, "Pretend that this empty field is your front yard. I want you to pick up all the trash in your yard that other people have left there."

She looked terribly confused, but just said, "How long do I have to do this for?"

"Until you get it," I said.

She shook her head and shrugged, then painstakingly picked up every cigarette butt, soda can, newspaper, potato chip bag, and other inorganic object she could find.

Anyone watching would have thought she was on a prison cleanup detail and I was her warden. But I wasn't being cruel to her, and this wasn't a punishment. Quite the contrary. I was setting her free. I didn't force her to do it; she could have quit at any time if she wanted to. However, she knew that if she quit on the activity she would be quitting on herself and would miss the breakthrough moment she had traveled far to experience.

We'd been out there in the cold rain for an hour and a half when she suddenly dropped the bag and started screaming, "I GOT IT! I GOT IT!" She ran over to me and gave me a huge bear hug.

"Thank you, Sean!"

"So what did you get?" I said with a smile.

"Well, a lot of things, actually." She was transformed. "I learned that even though other people may litter in our yard, it is our responsibility to clean it up. If we don't clean up our own yard, no one else ever will.

"I have spent my entire life blaming my father and dozens of other men for trashing my life," she continued. "I've never cleaned up what they left me, so I've left a big sign for other men that my yard is a trash dump they can toss their garbage on as much as they want."

She paused, looking sad. "I've turned my life into a landfill and blamed everyone for throwing their trash on me. I've attracted disgusting things into my life because I've never cleaned myself up. If you don't clean up a yard full of trash, you will breed diseases, smells, and god-awful sights. I'm responsible for my yard and for how it is kept. I am responsible for how I allow others to treat me.

When I was a kid," she said, "I didn't know any better than to tolerate abuse. I'm an adult now. I can take out the trash from my past and have a clean yard again." She shook her head, smiling again.

"Thank you, Sean."

"*You're* the one that you should be thanking, not me."

She laughed.

"I have one last step for you. I want you to visualize your favorite meal on the planet."

She closed her eyes and smiled. "Okay, I'm picturing it right now."

"Perfect. Now, would you ever want to put that meal inside that bag of trash you're holding?"

She looked at the bag in disgust and said, "Hell, no! That would be ridiculous."

"Exactly. I want you to remember that when you go home. Never place what you love—yourself—in an environment of trash."

"I won't," she said. Then she went quiet for a minute. Clearly, something had just occurred to her.

"I guess I have to stop feeling sorry for myself, don't I?"

GET OFF YOUR BUT *NOW!*
What Trash Are You Holding on to?

It's time to get your hands dirty. Ready to do some work?

In your Get Off Your BUT Now! journal, make a list of five people or events that you have allowed to litter your yard for too long.

When you take out the trash that's been littering your life, you will make room for positive change to occur. Until you stop living on the Effect side of the equation, no quantity of "self-help" books, seminars, and coaching will help you.

Self-Pity Is a Drug

You will never be living at Cause until you stop blaming other people for what is wrong in your life. This means giving up the pleasure you derive from self-pity. Don't act as if you don't know what I'm talking about!

Pity is a drug. Your first hit on the pity pipe makes you feel good, but it's just a temporary fix. All too soon, it leaves you in a darker place, craving more.

The woman who blamed her father's abuse for ruining her life had gotten years of gratification from sucking on her pity pipe. When she finally realized that her self-pity was getting her nowhere, she got some help. Until she *owned* the result—she'd allowed other men to trash her life too—she couldn't move on. When she began cleaning her (metaphorical) yard, she learned that it was up to her to keep it clean. She stopped feeling sorry for herself and was able to move on to healthier relationships.

Setting down your pity pipe isn't comfortable or easy. At first you may feel the anger, sadness, or confusion that your pity has been dulling all these years. You'll experience some withdrawal pains for a while, but it is the only way you will ever truly own your life and begin living at Cause.

GET OFF YOUR BUT *NOW!*
Put Down Your Pity Pipe

In your Get Off Your BUT *Now!* journal, write down the names of five people you blame for all the things that have gone wrong in your life.

Forgiving these people is the key to your living salvation. You don't have to condone their actions to let them out of your head. You *do* have to absolve them of responsibility for your life.

Here's a condensed version of a process of forgiveness that the Hawaiian tradition calls *Ho'oponopono*. In your mind's eye, call each person up onto a stage, one at a time. Share with him that you are done being controlled by him, that you are done living in anger, sadness, guilt, and fear because of him. Tell him that for this reason, you need to cut the energetic chord that ties the two of you together. Apologize to him for making him wrong and bad. Tell him that you realize that he did the best he could with what he had. Let him know you forgive him for all the wrong that you feel he had done to you.

This will not be easy. If you don't feel ready to do this activity, I respect those feelings.

The Power of Cause

Living at Cause may seem like a difficult thing to do. It is—at first. When you live at Cause, you can't pass the buck. You can't get out of doing the tough stuff. Ultimately, however, you will be granted access to a world most people can experience only vicariously. You get to be the star of your own movie, instead of fading into the crowd of faceless extras.

When I was first starting my business, I spent literally hundreds of days blaming outside forces for my tough financial times. I'd blame the economy, my prospects, and even my industry. I was so busy looking for a scapegoat that I had no time to actually grab the bull by the horns. Then I heard a mentor of mine, Larry Winget, tell a crowd of business executives, "The economy doesn't suck—you suck!"

I was blown back in my chair. That was pretty abrasive! What was this guy talking about? As he continued his talk, however, he shared example after example of companies and corporate executives who manage to make billions of dollars during tough economic times. People get rich, he explained, when they "Shut up, stop whining, and get a life!"

Ding!

I was painfully reminded of the sound the egg timer made when my childhood pity party was finally over. I wasn't using my creativity and work ethic to develop a solution; I was using it to develop the problem. I had become my own energy vampire. *Unacceptable!*

This was a rude awakening in my career, and a real turning point in my business life.

I shared my revelation with Mike, my mentor-friend (I call him my friendtor). He just said, "It's about time you saw what all your friends have been telling you."

"What?" I was honestly puzzled.

"Sean," said Mike, "you *talk* a lot about what you're going to do with your business. You need to start producing the results."

Ouch! Comments like that don't sit well with anyone, let alone a person who thought he was a professional motivator. I couldn't argue with him—he was right. I was living at Effect in my business, and there was no hiding it.

I'm going to take the gloves off here. You can pretend to the world as much as you want that you've got it all together, disguising yourself as a fitness buff who has lots of money and a great job and a great relationship. But when you put your head on the pillow every night, you know full well that you're unhappy with what you weigh, how much money is in your bank account, the sorry state of your romantic and emotional relationships—and the enormous amount of energy you have to put out every minute of every day to keep the world from finding out what a fraud you are.

Don't kid yourself. Anyone with sensory acuity can see what's going on.

The Wheel-Catching Moment

Once I stopped talking about action and started *taking* action in my business, everything turned around. Not overnight, of course. I had to work on what I wanted and wait for the results. I call this the wheel-catching moment.

When a driver of a car turns the steering wheel, there's a time delay before the tires head in the new direction. Our lives follow the same principle. You can't safely lose fifty pounds overnight. You can't (normally) get out of $100,000 debt in an hour. And you can't fix a failing relationship in a day. It took you months if not years of living at Effect (stuck on your BUT) to get you into those health, wealth, and relationship predicaments—you can't expect to get out of them overnight. You *can* expect to see results when you decide to take ownership of your life. You just have to have patience and faith in yourself.

Here's one more story for you. When I was in college, I was super frustrated with having to take courses on subjects that I didn't enjoy. At one point, I considered dropping out of school completely and running my speaking business full-time, a decision my parents were totally against.

So I decided to talk to Tony Robbins about it. I thought, *He never went to college, and look how successful he is.* I was sure he would side with me. Boy, am I glad he didn't.

Tony said, "Sean, being a college dropout isn't a convincing sell as a motivational speaker to the education industry you often speak in. You never know where your college degree will take you. You're so close. Just hang in there. Besides," he said, "I've found that focusing on your one-year goals will drive you nuts. You'll be amazed with what you can do with your five- and ten-year goals. If you respect my opinion like you say you do, stay in school."

Crud. I thought for sure he would see my side. So I stuck out school and graduated with high honors.

Here's why I'm glad he stood his ground and told me what he did. If I had dropped out of college, I would never have been able to go on to become a therapist and certainly wouldn't have been able to enroll in a PhD program. Of course, my parents had told me exactly the same thing Tony told me, but I didn't believe them. Why? Because I'm human, and humans take advice from their pit crew more than they listen to any other group of people.

Can you imagine if I had turned to my C Friends for advice on this decision? Takers, energy drainers, and destroyers would have given me awful advice. "Just quit, Sean!" I can't allow that for myself. Neither can you.

Living at Cause will immunize you from the "BUT it's not fair" disease. You'll be able to look at everything that happens and know that it serves you either as a reward for your effort or as a learning experience for a course correction. This is the open secret about why I'm so content with my life. I believe that I'm responsible for handling anything that falls in my yard. That means I can feel deserving of the money I make, the women I attract, the accomplishments I rack up, and all the amazing people I have in my pit crew. No good thing happens to me by accident—not in my self-appointed reality.

On the flip side, I understand that anything in my life that I don't like—anything that's uncomfortable, inconvenient, or even horrifying—is something that can teach me an extremely valuable life lesson.

The smallest things in life can grow into obstacles that bring us to our knees—if we don't pay attention and own them. Yet the simple act of owning them shrinks them back down to size.

I'm done with waking up every day, scared that life is just a chaotic game of chance. I see it as a beautiful living structure of opportunities that I bring into my existence. Could I be wrong? Sure. If an individual wanted to disprove my theory with logic, I'd let him speak his mind.

Then I would kindly ask him how happy he is, how much money he has in the bank, whether he is in a great romantic relationship, and whether he is in the shape that he wants to be in.

I'm sure he'd ask, "What the heck does that have to do with anything?"

To which I'd reply, "I don't take advice from someone who doesn't have what I want."

I would ask myself, *Is this man a skeptic or a cynic?* Skeptics are individuals trying to make sense of everything. I like skeptics. They are open to believing new things if evidence is produced showing that they are wrong. Cynics, in contrast, are looking to prove that they are right. If you produce evidence that they are wrong, they will either run away, attack you, or throw a tantrum. I don't take this personally. If anything, I thank them for appearing in my reality, for teaching me that I am exactly where I want to be in my life—on the Cause side of the equation.

You Choose

People often ask me if I guarantee results with my clients. My answer is, yes and no. Yes, I guarantee that by the end of our session they will achieve the goal that they set at the beginning of the session. They will experience a personal breakthrough moment of clarity, inspiration, self-realization, or personal resolve with their past. If, by the end of the session, they don't believe they've received that experience, I will give them a full refund. However, I do not guarantee what will happen once they leave my office.

What?

It's my job to assist clients in letting go of their limiting beliefs and negative emotions, and help them release the firm grasp they have on the problem in their mind that is responsible for manifesting all the external problems in their life. That's it. Once they leave me, however, they are responsible for everything else.

Is it going to be easy? Of course not. That's why I equip my clients with the tools and mind-set they need to navigate life once they leave my office. It's not a matter of being perfect; it's a matter of no longer repeating past negative behaviors once you realize that they've been running your life. It may sound harsh, but here's what I've found:

If they choose not to use the connection techniques I taught them, they'll continue to struggle.

If they go home and keep talking to themselves like an enemy, beating themselves up at every turn, they'll continue to struggle.

If they take on the body language of someone afraid of her own shadow, they'll continue to struggle.

If they focus on all the things they don't want and don't have and that aren't fair, they'll continue to struggle.

If they go back to their negative pit crew and do nothing to change it, they'll continue to struggle.

If they choose to blame everyone and his dog for their problems, living at Effect . . . you can finish the sentence by now.

My Breakthrough Process only works if you do your assignments. And that's why I don't guarantee anything once clients leave my office. I'm not in the business of babysitting victims. I'm in the business of teaching people how to be victors. I show people how to get off their BUTS and make something of their lives. What they do with these teachings and demonstrations comes down to them.

I wish I had a magic wand; I could wave it over your head, say, "Get off your BUT *now!*" and have it be so. I don't. This book is the closest thing I have to that wand. Don't get me wrong—there is magic in these pages. It's up to you to apply the lessons and do the activities. If you just read this book passively, prepare for passive results. If you work the lessons actively, choosing to live at Cause—watch out, world!

The information in this book is in your hands now; what you choose to do with it is up to you.

One Last Thing...

Allow me to leave you with this parting piece of wisdom. One of my mentors, Eben Pagan, once asked me, "Sean, when does a person learn something?"

I thought about it, and said, "When they retain the information they set forth to absorb."

"Wrong," he replied. "Learning doesn't occur until a behavior has changed. As long as you know something intellectually but you have yet to put it into practice, you haven't learned it at all."

Whoa!

I chewed on that conversation for months. I looked at my own life, and saw that what Eben had told me was true. I looked at the lives of my pit crew, and saw his words to be true there too. I looked at my clients and people I had met on my speaking tours, and found it to be true for them as well.

Huh? I guess common sense isn't common sense until it is common *practice*.

Put the knowledge of this book into practice. Go out there and get the results you've always thought and talked about having. Show the world that you're doing the bravest, smartest, and most productive thing a person can do—getting off your BUT and *taking a stand* for your life!

RESOURCES

My Private Practice
For more information on my private sessions and my Breakthrough Process, visit my Web site:

www.BreakthroughWithSean.com

Books That Shaped My Life
Read the books that influenced me and helped me get off my BUT:

Paulo Coelho, *The Alchemist*

Susan Jeffers, *Feel the Fear . . . and Do It Anyway*

Robert Maurer, *One Small Step*

Dan Millman, *Way of the Peaceful Warrior*

Steven Pressfield, *The War of Art*

don Miguel Ruiz, *The Four Agreements* and *The Mastery of Love*

Eckhart Tolle, *A New Earth*

Neal Donald Walsch, *Conversations with God*

Music That Shaped My Life

When my BUTS weigh me down, I often turn to music. The greatest of musicians to have ever inspired, uplifted, and motivated me is award-winning singer-songwriter Tiamo De Vettori. Visit his Web site:

www.TiamoMusic.com

Movies That Shaped My Life

If you love movies as much as I do—and even if you don't!—these are worth your time.

Contact

The Matrix

Peaceful Warrior

Phenomenon

Powder

The Secret

Online Resources

I am grateful to my friends who contributed their inspiring true stories for this book. If you'd like to learn more about them, please visit their Web sites:

Andréa Albright: www.AndreaAlbright.com

Peter Bielagus: www.PeterBSpeaks.com

Mike Domitrz: www.MikeDomitrz.com

Rene Godefroy: www.ReneGodefroy.com

Bobby Petrocelli: www.BobbyPetrocelli.com

Mind

I got off my BUT excuses, insecurities, and fears that were weighing me down *emotionally* by attending the live events and purchasing the products from these sites:

Tony Robbins: www.TonyRobbins.com

Landmark Education: www.LandmarkEducation.com

The Empowerment Partnership: www.NLP.com

Body

I got off my BUT excuses, insecurities, and fears that were weighing me down *physically* by attending the live events and purchasing the products from these sites:

pH Miracle Living: www.pHMiracleLiving.com

Fit Speakers: www.FitSpeakers.com

Amazing Body Now: www.AmazingBodyNow.com

Spirit

I got off my BUT excuses, insecurities, and fears that were weighing me down *spiritually* by attending the live events and purchasing the products from these sites:

The Work of Byron Katie: www.TheWork.com

Dr. Wayne Dyer: www.DrWayneDyer.com

The Secret: www.TheSecret.tv

Dating Advice for Men

I created a resource for any guy who wants to get off the BUTS that are holding him back in attracting the women he wants. This site develops a guy into a man who naturally attracts women (even if he wants to attract his current wife or girlfriend). Visit *Inner Game Magazine:*

www.InnerGameMagazine.com

Dating Advice for Women

My close friend Christian Carter has an amazing set of tools that I personally endorse for any woman who wants to get off her BUT and attract and keep the guy of her dreams. Visit Christian's Web site:

www.ChristianCarter.com

Sex Advice

My close friend Alex Allman is one of the best experts on how to get off those BUTS that are stopping you from having an amazing and healthy sexual life with your partner. Visit him at his Web site:

www.RevolutionarySex.com

Small Business Advice

My close friend Christian Mickelsen has one of the most "resource-full" Web sites for people who are held back by their BUTS in growing their small business. Visit his Web site:

www.SmallBizU.com

THE AUTHOR

Sean Clinch Stephenson is one of the leading authorities on the deconstruction of self-sabotage (what he calls getting people off their BUTS). A psychotherapist and internationally known professional speaker, Sean has been sharing his findings with audiences since 1996, at corporations, places of worship, educational institutions, correctional facilities, wellness conferences, sales trainings, leadership retreats, and health care facilities. He publishes the international men's online magazine InnerGameMagazine.com, is completing his PhD in clinical hypnosis at American Pacific University, and has a private psychotherapy practice in Oakbrook Terrace, Illinois.